Miscellany Poems on Several Occasions by Anne Kingsmill Finch

The Countess of Winchilsea

Anne Kingsmill was born in April 1661 (an exact date is not known) in Sydmonton, Hampshire.

Throughout her life Anne was involved in several Court cases that dragged on for years. These involved both a share of her parents estate for her education and later her and her husband's share of an inheritance.

In 1682, Anne became a maid of honour to Mary of Modena (wife of James, Duke of York, later King James II) at St James's Palace.

Anne's interest in poetry began at the palace, and she started writing her own verse. The Court however was no place for a woman to display any poetic efforts. Woman were not considered suitable for such literary pursuits.

At court, Anne met Colonel Heneage Finch. A courtier as well as a soldier. The couple married on 15th May 1684.

Index of Content

I0145567

THE BOOKSELLER TO THE READER

The Town having already done Justice to the Ode on the SPLEEN, and some few Pieces in this Volume, when scattered in other Miscellanies: I think it will be sufficient (now that Permission is at last obtained for the Printing this Collection) to acquaint the Reader, that they are of the same Hand; which I doubt not will render this Miscellany an acceptable Present to the Publick.

MERCURY and the ELEPHANT

A Prefatory FABLE

As Merc'ry travell'd thro' a Wood,
(Whose Errands are more Fleet than Good)
An Elephant before him lay,
That much encumber'd had the Way:
The Messenger, who's still in haste,
Wou'd fain have bow'd, and so have past;
When up arose th' unweildy Brute,
And wou'd repeat a late Dispute,
In which (he said) he'd gain'd the Prize
From a wild Boar of monstrous Size:
But Fame (quoth he) with all her Tongues,
Who Lawyers, Ladies, Soldiers wrongs,
Has, to my Disadvantage, told
An Action throughly Bright and Bold;
Has said, that I foul Play had us'd,
And with my Weight th' Opposer bruis'd;
Had laid my Trunk about his Brawn,
Before his Tushes cou'd be drawn;
Had stunn'd him with a hideous Roar,
And twenty-thousand Scandals more:
But I defy the Talk of Men,
Or Voice of Brutes in ev'ry Den;

Th' impartial Skies are all my Care,
And how it stands Recorded there.
Amongst you Gods, pray, What is thought?
  Quoth Mercury—Then have you Fought!

  Solicitous thus shou'd I be
For what's said of my Verse and Me;
Or shou'd my Friends Excuses frame,
And beg the Criticks not to blame
(Since from a Female Hand it came)
Defects in Judgment, or in Wit;
They'd but reply—Then has she Writ!

  Our Vanity we more betray,
In asking what the World will say,
Than if, in trivial Things like these,
We wait on the Event with ease;
Nor make long Prefaces, to show
What Men are not concern'd to know:
For still untouch'd how we succeed,
'Tis for themselves, not us, they Read;
Whilst that proceeding to requite,
We own (who in the Muse delight)
'Tis for our Selves, not them, we Write.
Betray'd by Solitude to try
Amusements, which the Prosp'rous fly;
And only to the Press repair,
To fix our scatter'd Papers there;
Tho' whilst our Labours are preserv'd,
The Printers may, indeed, be starv'd.

All is Vanity

I

How vain is Life! which rightly we compare
  To flying Posts, that haste away;
To Plants, that fade with the declining Day;
  To Clouds, that sail amidst the yielding Air;
Till by Extention into that they flow,
  Or, scatt'ring on the World below,
Are lost and gone, ere we can say they were;
  To Autumn-leaves, which every Wind can chace;
To rising Bubbles, on the Waters Face;
  To fleeting Dreams, that will not stay,
Nor in th' abused Fancy dance,

When the returning Rays of Light,
Resuming their alternate Right,
Break on th' ill-order'd Scene on the fantastick Trance:
As weak is Man, whilst Tenant to the Earth;
As frail and as uncertain all his Ways,
From the first moment of his weeping Birth,
Down to the last and best of his few restless Days;
　When to the Land of Darkness he retires
From disappointed Hopes, and frustrated Desires;
　Reaping no other Fruit of all his Pain
Bestow'd whilst in the vale of Tears below,
　But this unhappy Truth, at last to know,
That Vanity's our Lot, and all Mankind is Vain.

II

If past the hazard of his tendrest Years,
　Neither in thoughtless Sleep opprest,
　Nor poison'd with a tainted Breast,
Loos'd from the infant Bands and female Cares,
　A studious Boy, advanc'd beyond his Age,
Wastes the dim Lamp, and turns the restless Page;
　For some lov'd Book prevents the rising Day,
　And on it, stoln aside, bestows the Hours of Play;
Him the observing Master do's design
For search of darkned Truths and Mysteries Divine;
　Bids him with unremitted Labour trace
The Rise of Empires, and their various Fates,
The several Tyrants o'er the several States,
　To Babel's lofty Towers, and warlike Nimrod's Race;
Bids him in Paradice the Bank survey,
　Where Man, new-moulded from the temper'd Clay,
(Till fir'd with Breath Divine) a helpless Figure lay:
　Could he be led thus far---What were the Boast,
　What the Reward of all the Toil it cost,
What from that Land of ever-blooming Spring,
　For our Instruction could he bring,
Unless, that having Humane Nature found
Unseparated from its Parent Ground,
　(Howe'er we vaunt our Elevated Birth)
　The Epicure in soft Array,
　The lothsome Beggar, that before
His rude unhospitable Door,
　Unpity'd but by Brutes, a broken Carcass lay,
Were both alike deriv'd from the same common Earth?
　But ere the Child can to these Heights attain,
　Ere he can in the Learned Sphere arise;

A guilding Star, attracting to the Skies,
A fever, seizing the o'er labour'd Brain,
  Sends him, perhaps, to Death's concealing Shade;
Where, in the Marble Tomb now silent laid,
  He better do's that useful Doctrine show,
  (Which all the sad Assistants ought to know,
  Who round the Grave his short continuance mourn)
That first from Dust we came, and must to Dust return.

III

A bolder Youth, grown capable of Arms,
Bellona courts with her prevailing Charms;
  Bids th' inchanting Trumpet sound,
  Loud as Triumph, soft as Love,
  Striking now the Poles above,
  Then descending from the Skies,
  Soften every falling Note;
As the harmonious Lark that sings and flies,
When near the Earth, contracts her narrow Throat,
  And warbles on the Ground:
Shews the proud Steed, impatient of the Check,
  'Gainst the loudest Terrors Proof,
Pawing the Valley with his steeled Hoof,
With Lightning arm'd his Eyes, with Thunder cloth'd his Neck;
  Who on the th' advanced Foe, (the Signal giv'n)
Flies, like a rushing Storm by mighty Whirlwinds driv'n;
  Lays open the Records of Fame,
No glorious Deed omits, no Man of mighty Name;
  Their Stratagems, their Tempers she'll repeat,
  From Alexander's, (truly stil'd the GREAT)
  From Cæsar's on the World's Imperial Seat,
  To Turenne's Conduct, and to Conde's Heat.
'Tis done! and now th' ambitious Youth disdains
  The safe, but harder Labours of the Gown,
  The softer pleasures of the Courtly Town,
The once lov'd rural Sports, and Chaces on the Plains;
  Does with the Soldier's Life the Garb assume,
  The gold Embroid'ries, and the graceful Plume;
  Walks haughty in a Coat of Scarlet Die,
  A Colour well contriv'd to cheat the Eye,
Where richer Blood, alas! may undistinguisht lye.
  And oh! too near that wretched Fate attends;
  Hear it ye Parents, all ye weeping Friends!
  Thou fonder Maid! won by these gaudy Charms,
  (The destin'd Prize of his Victorious Arms)
  Now fainting Dye upon the mournful Sound,

That speaks his hasty Death, and paints the fatal Wound!
  Trail all your Pikes, dispirit every Drum,
  March in a slow Procession from afar,
  Ye silent, ye dejected Men of War!
  Be still the Hautboys, and the Flute be dumb!
  Display no more, in vain, the lofty Banner;
  For see! where on the Bier before ye lies
  The pale, the fall'n, th' untimely Sacrifice
To your mistaken Shrine, to your false Idol Honour!

IV

  As Vain is Beauty, and as short her Power;
  Tho' in its proud, and transitory Sway,
  The coldest Hearts and wisest Heads obey
  That gay fantastick Tyrant of an Hour.
  On Beauty's Charms, (altho' a Father's Right,
  Tho' grave Seleucus! to thy Royal Side
  By holy Vows fair Stratonice be ty'd)
  With anxious Joy, with dangerous Delight,
  Too often gazes thy unwary Son,
  Till past all Hopes, expiring and undone,
  A speaking Pulse the secret Cause impart;
  The only time, when the Physician's Art
Could ease that lab'ring Grief, or heal a Lover's Smart.
  See Great Antonius now impatient stand,
    Expecting, with mistaken Pride,
  On Cydnus crowded Shore, on Cydnus fatal Strand,
  A Queen, at his Tribunal to be try'd,
  A Queen that arm'd in Beauty, shall deride
  His feeble Rage, and his whole Fate command:
  O'er the still Waves her burnisht Galley moves,
  Row'd by the Graces, whilst officious Loves
  To silken Cords their busie Hands apply,
  Or gathering all the gentle Gales that fly,
  To their fair Mistress with these Spoils repair,
And from their purple Wings disperse the balmy Air.
  Hov'ring Perfumes ascend in od'rous Clouds,
  Curl o'er the Barque, and play among the Shrouds;
Whilst gently dashing every Silver Oar,
  Guided by the Rules of Art,
  With tuneful Instruments design'd
To soften, and subdue the stubborn Mind,
A strangely pleasing and harmonious Part
  In equal Measures bore.
Like a new Venus on her native Sea,
  In midst of the transporting Scene,

(Which Pen or Pencil imitates in vain)
On a resplendent and conspicuous Bed,
With all the Pride of Persia loosely spread,
　The lovely Syrene lay.
　Which but discern'd from the yet distant Shore,
　Th' amazed Emperor could hate no more;
　No more a baffled Vengeance could pursue;
　But yielding still, still as she nearer drew,
　When Cleopatra anchor'd in the Bay,
　Where every Charm cou'd all its Force display,
Like his own Statue stood, and gaz'd the World away.

　Where ends alas! this Pageantry and State;
　Where end the Triumphs of this conqu'ring Face,
Envy'd of Roman Wives, and all the Female Race?
　Oh swift Vicissitude of Beauty's Fate!
　Now in her Tomb withdrawn from publick Sight,
　　From near Captivity and Shame,
　　The vanquish'd, the abandon'd Dame
　Proffers the Arm, that held another's Right,
　To the destructive Snake's more just Embrace,
And courts deforming Death, to mend his Leaden Pace.

V

　But Wit shall last (the vaunting Poet cries)
　Th' immortal Streams that from Parnassus flow,
　Shall make his never-fading Lawrels grow,
Above this mouldring Earth to flourish in the Skies:
"And when his Body falls in Funeral Fire,
　When late revolving Ages shall consume
　The very Pillars, that support his Tomb,
"His name shall live, and his best Part aspire.
　Deluded Wretch! grasping at future Praise,
　　Now planting, with mistaken Care,
　Round thy enchanted Palace in the Air,
　A Grove, which in thy Fancy time shall raise,
　A Grove of soaring Palms, and everlasting Bays;
　Could'st Thou alas! to such Reknown arrive,
　As thy Imagination wou'd contrive;
　Should numerous Cities, in a vain contest,
　　Struggle for thy famous Birth;
Should the sole Monarch of the conquer'd Earth,
　His wreathed Head upon thy Volume rest;
　　Like Maro, could'st thou justly claim,
　　Amongst th' inspired tuneful Race,
　The highest Room, the undisputed Place;

And after near Two Thousand Years of Fame,
    Have thy proud Work to a new People shown;
      Th' unequal'd Poems made their own,
    In such a Dress, in such a perfect Stile
    As on his Labours Dryden now bestows,
    As now from Dryden's just Improvement flows,
In every polish'd Verse throughout the British Isle;
    What Benefit alas! would to thee grow?
      What Sense of Pleasure wou'dst thou know?
    What swelling Joy? what Pride? what Glory have,
    When in the Darkness of the abject Grave,
    Insensible, and Stupid laid below,
    No Atom of thy Heap, no Dust wou'd move,
For all the airy Breath that form'd thy Praise above?

VI

    True, says the Man to Luxury inclin'd;
    Without the Study of uncertain Art,
      Without much Labour of the Mind,
    Meer uninstructed Nature will impart,
That Life too swiftly flies, and leaves all good behind.
    Sieze then, my Friends, (he cries) the present Hour;
      The Pleasure which to that belongs,
    The Feasts, th' o'erflowing Bowls, the Mirth, the Songs,
    The Orange-Bloom, that with such Sweetness blows,
      Anacreon's celebrated Rose,
    The Hyacinth, with every beauteous Flower,
    Which just this happy Moment shall disclose,
Are out of Fortune's reach, and all within our Power.
    Such costly Garments let our Slaves prepare,
    As for the gay Demetrius were design'd;
    Where a new Sun of radiant Diamonds shin'd,
Where the enamel'd Earth, and scarce-discerned Air,
      With a transparent Sea were seen,
    A Sea composed of the Em'rald's Green,
    And with a golden Shore encompass'd round;
Where every Orient Shell, of wondrous shape was found.
    The whole Creation on his Shoulders hung,
    The whole Creation with his Wish comply'd,
Did swiftly, for each Appetite provide,
    And fed them all when Young.
    No less, th' Assyrian Prince enjoy'd,
Of Bliss too soon depriv'd, but never cloy'd,
    Whose Counsel let us still pursue,
Whose Monument, did this Inscription shew
    To every Passenger, that trod the way,

Where, with a slighting Hand, and scornful Smile
The proud Effigies, on th' instructive Pile,
  A great Example lay.
I, here Entomb'd, did mighty Kingdoms sway,
Two Cities rais'd in one prodigious Day:
Thou wand'ring Traveller, no longer gaze,
No longer dwell upon this useless Place;
Go Feed, and Drink, in Sports consume thy Life;
For All that else we gain's not worth a Moment's Strife.
  Thus! talks the Fool, whom no Restraint can bound,
  When now the Glass has gone a frequent round;
    When soaring Fancy lightly swims,
  Fancy, that keeps above, and dances o'er the Brims;
  Whilst weighty Reason sinks, and in the bottom's drown'd;
  Adds to his Own, an artificial Fire,
    Doubling ev'ry hot Desire,
  Till th' auxiliary Spirits, in a Flame,
  The Stomach's Magazine defy,
  That standing Pool, that helpless Moisture nigh,
  Thro' every Vital part impetuous fly,
    And quite consume the Frame;
  When to the Under-world despis'd he goes,
  A pamper'd Carcase on the Worms bestows,
  Who rioting on the unusual Chear,
As good a Life enjoy, as he could boast of here.

VII

  But hold my Muse! thy farther Flight restrain,
    Exhaust not thy declining Force,
  Nor in a long, pursu'd, and breathless Course,
    Attempt, with slacken'd speed, to run
  Through ev'ry Vanity beneath the Sun,
  Lest thy o'erweary'd Reader, should complain,
    That of all Vanities beside,
  Which thine, or his Experience e'er have try'd,
Thou art, too tedious Muse, most frivolous and vain;
  Yet, tell the Man, of an aspiring Thought,
    Of an ambitious, restless Mind,
  That can no Ease, no Satisfaction find,
  Till neighb'ring States are to Subjection brought,
Till Universal Awe, enslav'd Mankind is taught;
  That, should he lead an Army to the Field,
    For whose still necessary Use,
  Th' extended Earth cou'd not enough produce,
Nor Rivers to their Thirst a full Contentment yield;
  Yet, must their dark Reverse of Fate

Roll round, within that Course of Years,
Within the short, the swift, and fleeting Date
Prescrib'd by Xerxes, when his falling Tears
Bewail'd those Numbers, which his Sword employ'd,
And false, Hyena-like, lamented and destroy'd.
Tell Him, that does some stately Building raise,
   A Windsor or Versailles erect,
And thorough all Posterity expect,
With its unshaken Base, a firm unshaken Praise;
Tell Him, Judea's Temple is no more,
Upon whose Splendour, Thousands heretofore
Spent the astonish'd Hours, forgetful to Adore:
Tell him, into the Earth agen is hurl'd,
That most stupendious Wonder of the World,
Justly presiding o'er the boasted Seven,
By humane Art and Industry design'd,
This! the rich Draught of the Immortal Mind,
   The Architect of Heaven.
Remember then, to fix thy Aim on High,
Project, and build on t'other side the Sky,
For, after all thy vain Expence below,
Thou canst no Fame, no lasting Pleasure know;
No Good, that shall not thy Embraces fly;
Or thou from that be in a Moment caught,
Thy Spirit to new Claims, new Int'rests brought,
Whilst unconcern'd thy secret Ashes lye,
Or stray about the Globe, O Man ordain'd to Dye!

The Prevalence of Custom

A Female, to a Drunkard marry'd,
When all her other Arts miscarry'd,
Had yet one Stratagem to prove him,
And from good Fellowship remove him;
Finding him overcome with Tipple,
And weak, as Infant at the Nipple,
She to a Vault transports the Lumber,
And there expects his breaking Slumber.
A Table she with Meat provided,
And rob'd in Black, stood just beside it;
Seen only, by one glim'ring Taper,
That blewly burnt thro' misty Vapor.
At length he wakes, his Wine digested,
And of her Phantomship requested,
To learn the Name of that close Dwelling,
And what offends his Sight and Smelling;

And of what Land she was the Creature,
With outspread Hair, and ghastly Feature?
Mortal, quoth she, (to Darkness hurry'd)
Know, that thou art both Dead and Bury'd;
Convey'd, last Night, from noisie Tavern,
To this thy still, and dreary Cavern.
What strikes thy Nose, springs from the Shatters
Of Bodies kill'd with Cordial Waters,
Stronger than other Scents and quicker,
As urg'd by more spirituous Liquor.
My self attend on the Deceas'd,
When all their Earthly Train's releas'd;
And in this Place of endless Quiet,
My Bus'ness is, to find them Diet;
To shew all sorts of Meats, and Salades,
Till I'm acquainted with their Palates;
But that once known, then less suffices.
Quoth he (and on his Crupper rises)
Thou Guardian of these lower Regions,
Thou Providor for countless Legions,
Thou dark, but charitable Crony,
Far kinder than my Tisiphony,
Who of our Victuals thus art Thinking,
If thou hast Care too of our Drinking,
A Bumper fetch: Quoth she, a Halter,
Since nothing less thy Tone can alter,
Or break this Habit thou'st been getting,
To keep thy Throat in constant wetting.

The Mussulman's Dream OF THE VIZIER and DERVIS

Where is that World, to which the Fancy flies,
When Sleep excludes the Present from our Eyes;
Whose Map no Voyager cou'd e'er design,
Nor to Description its wild Parts confine?
Yet such a Land of Dreams We must allow,
Who nightly trace it, tho' we know not how:
Unfetter'd by the Days obtruded Rules,
We All enjoy that Paradise of Fools;
And find a Sorrow, in resuming Sense,
Which breaks some free Delight,
And snatches us from thence.
  Thus! in a Dream, a Musselman was shown
A Vizir, whom he formerly had known,
When at the Port he bore deputed Sway,
And made the Nations with a Nod obey.

Now all serene, and splendid was his Brow,
Whilst ready Waiters to his Orders bow;
His Residence, an artful Garden seem'd,
Adorn'd with all, that pleasant he esteem'd;
Full of Reward, his glorious Lot appear'd,
As with the Sight, our Dreamer's Mind was chear'd;
But turning, next he saw a dreadful Sight,
Which fill'd his Soul with Wonder and Affright,
Pursu'd by Fiends, a wretched Dervis fled
Through scorching Plains, which to wide Distance spread;
Whilst every Torture, gloomy Poets paint,
Was there prepar'd for the reputed Saint.
Amaz'd at this, the sleeping Turk enquires,
Why He that liv'd above, in soft Attires,
Now roll'd in Bliss, while t'other roll'd in Fires?
We're taught the Suff'rings of this Future State,
Th' Excess of Courts is likeliest to create;
Whilst solitary Cells, o'ergrown with Shade,
The readiest way to Paradise is made.
True, quoth the Phantom (which he dream'd reply'd)
The lonely Path is still the surest Guide,
Nor is it by these Instances deny'd.
For, know my Friend, whatever Fame report,
The Vizier to Retirements wou'd resort,
Th' ambitious Dervis wou'd frequent the Court.

The Shepherd Piping to the Fishes

A Shepherd seeking with his Lass
  To shun the Heat of Day;
Was seated on the shadow'd Grass,
Near which a flowing Stream did pass,
  And Fish within it play.
The Phillis he an Angle gave,
  And bid her toss the Line;
For sure, quoth he, each Fish must have,
Who do's not seek to be thy Slave,
  A harder Heart than mine.
Assemble here you watry Race,
  Transportedly he cries;
And if, when you behold her Face,
You e'er desire to quit the Place,
  You see not with my Eyes.
But you, perhaps, are by the Ear,
  More easie to be caught;
If so, I have my Bagpipe here,

The only Musick that's not dear,
  Nor in great Cities bought.
So sprightly was the Tune he chose,
  And often did repeat;
That Phillis, tho' not up she rose,
Kept time with every thrilling Close,
  And jigg'd upon her Seat.
But not a Fish wou'd nearer draw,
  No Harmony or Charms,
Their frozen Blood, it seems, cou'd thaw,
Nor all they heard, nor all they saw
  Cou'd woo them to such Terms.
The angry Shepherd in a Pett,
  Gives o'er his wheedling Arts,
And from his Shoulder throws the Net,
Resolv'd he wou'd a Supper get
  By Force, if not by Parts.
Thus stated Laws are always best
  To rule the vulgar Throng,
Who grow more Stubborn when Carest,
Or with soft Rhetorick addrest,
  If taking Measures wrong.

Love, Death, and Reputation

Reputation, Love, and Death,
(The Last all Bones, the First all Breath,
The Midd'st compos'd of Restless Fire)
From each other wou'd Retire;
Thro' the World resolv'd to stray;
Every One a several Way;
Exercising, as they went,
Each such Power, as Fate had lent;
Which, if it united were,
Wretched Mortals cou'd not bear:
But as parting Friends do show,
To what Place they mean to go,
Correspondence to engage,
Nominate their utmost Stage;
Death declar'd he wou'd be found
Near the fatal Trumpet's sound;
Or where Pestilences reign,
And Quacks the greater Plagues maintain;
Shaking still his sandy Glass,
And mowing Human Flesh, like Grass.
Love, as next his Leave he took,

Cast on both so sweet a Look,
As their Tempers near disarm'd,
One relax'd, and t'other warm'd;
Shades for his Retreat he chose,
Rural Plains, and soft Repose;
Where no Dowry e'er was paid,
Where no Jointure e'er was made;
No Ill Tongue the Nymph perplex'd,
Where no Forms the Shepherd vex'd;
Where Himself shou'd be the Care,
Of the Fond and of the Fair:
Where that was, they soon should know,
Au Revoir! then turn'd to Go.

Reputation made a Pause,
Suiting her severer Laws;
Second Thoughts, and Third she us'd,
Weighing Consequences mus'd;
When, at length to both she cry'd:
You Two safely may Divide,
To th' Antipodes may fall,
And re-ascend th' encompast Ball;
Certain still to meet agen
In the Breasts of tortur'd Men;
Who by One (too far) betray'd,
Call in t'other to their Aid:
Whilst I Tender, Coy, and Nice,
Rais'd and ruin'd in a Trice,
Either fix with those I grace,
Or abandoning the Place,
No Return my Nature bears,
From green Youth, or hoary Hairs;
If thro' Guilt, or Chance, I sever,
I once Parting, Part for ever.

There's No To-Morrow

A FABLE imitated from Sir Roger L'Estrange

Two long had Lov'd, and now the Nymph desir'd,
The Cloak of Wedlock, as the Case requir'd;
Urg'd that, the Day he wrought her to this Sorrow,
He Vow'd, that he wou'd marry her To-Morrow.
Agen he Swears, to shun the present Storm,
That he, To-Morrow, will that Vow perform.
The Morrows in their due Successions came;

Impatient still on Each, the pregnant Dame
Urg'd him to keep his Word, and still he swore the same.
When tir'd at length, and meaning no Redress,
But yet the Lye not caring to confess,
He for his Oath this Salvo chose to borrow,
That he was Free, since there was no To-Morrow;
For when it comes in Place to be employ'd,
'Tis then To-Day; To-Morrow's ne'er enjoy'd.
The Tale's a Jest, the Moral is a Truth;
To-Morrow and To-Morrow, cheat our Youth:
In riper Age, To-Morrow still we cry,
Not thinking, that the present Day we Dye;
Unpractis'd all the Good we had Design'd;
There's No To-Morrow to a Willing Mind.

The Petition for an Absolute Retreat.

Inscribed to the Right Honble CATHARINE Countess of THANET,

(Mention'd in the Poem under the Name of ARMINDA)

Give me O indulgent Fate!
Give me yet, before I Dye,
A sweet, but absolute Retreat,
'Mongst Paths so lost, and Trees so high,
That the World may ne'er invade,
Through such Windings and such Shade,
My unshaken Liberty.

  No Intruders thither come!
Who visit, but to be from home;
None who their vain Moments pass,
Only studious of their Glass,
News, that charm to listning Ears;
That false Alarm to Hopes and Fears;
That common Theme for every Fop,
From the Statesman to the Shop,
In those Coverts ne'er be spread,
Of who's Deceas'd, or who's to Wed,
Be no Tidings thither brought,
But Silent, as a Midnight Thought,
Where the World may ne'er invade,
Be those Windings, and that Shade:

  Courteous Fate! afford me there
A Table spread without my Care,

With what the neighb'ring Fields impart,
Whose Cleanliness be all it's Art,
When, of old, the Calf was drest,
(Tho' to make an Angel's Feast)
In the plain, unstudied Sauce
Nor Treufle, nor Morillia was;
Nor cou'd the mighty Patriarch's Board
One far-fetch'd Ortolano afford.
Courteous Fate, then give me there
Only plain, and wholesome Fare.
Fruits indeed (wou'd Heaven bestow)
All, that did in Eden grow,
All, but the Forbidden Tree,
Wou'd be coveted by me;
Grapes, with Juice so crouded up,
As breaking thro' the native Cup;
Figs (yet growing) candy'd o'er,
By the Sun's attracting Pow'r;
Cherries, with the downy Peach,
All within my easie Reach;
Whilst creeping near the humble Ground,
Shou'd the Strawberry be found
Springing wheresoe'er I stray'd,
Thro' those Windings and that Shade.

  For my Garments; let them be
What may with the Time agree;
Warm, when Phoebus does retire,
And is ill-supply'd by Fire:
But when he renews the Year,
And verdant all the Fields appear;
Beauty every thing resumes,
Birds have dropt their Winter-Plumes;
When the Lilly full display'd,
Stands in purer White array'd,
Than that Vest, which heretofore
The Luxurious Monarch wore,
When from Salem's Gates he drove,
To the soft Retreat of Love,
Lebanon's all burnish'd House,
And the dear Egyptian Spouse.
Cloath me, Fate, tho' not so Gay;
Cloath me light, and fresh as May:
In the Fountains let me view
All my Habit cheap and new;
Such as, when sweet Zephyrs fly,
With their Motions may comply;
Gently waving, to express

Unaffected Carelessness:
No Perfumes have there a Part,
Borrow'd from the Chymists Art:
But such as rise from flow'ry Beds,
Or the falling Jasmin Sheds!
'Twas the Odour of the Field,
Esau's rural Coat did yield,
That inspir'd his Father's Pray'r,
For Blessings of the Earth and Air:
Of Gums, or Pouders had it smelt;
The Supplanter, then unfelt,
Easily had been descry'd
For One that did in Tents abide;
For some beauteous Handmaids Joy,
And his Mother's darling Boy.
Let me then no Fragrance wear,
But what the Winds from Gardens bear,
In such kind, surprizing Gales,
As gather'd from Fidentia's Vales,
All the Flowers that in them grew;
Which intermixing, as they flew,
In wreathen Garlands dropt agen,
On Lucullus, and his Men;
Who, chear'd by the victorious Sight,
Trebl'd Numbers put to Flight.
Let me, when I must be fine,
In such natural Colours shine;
Wove, and painted by the Sun,
Whose resplendent Rays to shun,
When they do too fiercely beat,
Let me find some close Retreat,
Where they have no Passage made,
Thro' those Windings, and that Shade.

   Give me there (since Heaven has shown
It was not Good to be alone)
A Partner suited to my Mind,
Solitary, pleas'd and kind;
Who, partially, may something see
Preferr'd to all the World in me;
Slighting, by my humble Side,
Fame and Splendor, Wealth and Pride.
When but Two the Earth possest,
'Twas their happiest Days, and best;
They by Bus'ness, nor by Wars,
They by no Domestick Cares,
From each other e'er were drawn,
But in some Grove, or flow'ry Lawn,

Spent the swiftly flying Time,
Spent their own, and Nature's Prime,
In Love; that only Passion given
To perfect Man, whilst Friends with Heaven.
Rage, and Jealousie, and Hate,
Transports of his fallen State,
(When by Satan's Wiles betray'd)
Fly those Windings, and that Shade!

  Thus from Crouds, and Noise remov'd,
Let each Moment be improv'd;
Every Object still produce,
Thoughts of Pleasure, and of Use:
When some River slides away,
To encrease the boundless Sea;
Think we then, how Time do's haste,
To grow Eternity at last,
By the Willows, on the Banks,
Gather'd into social Ranks,
Playing with the gentle Winds,
Strait the Boughs, and smooth the Rinds,
Moist each Fibre, and each Top,
Wearing a luxurious Crop,
Let the time of Youth be shown,
The time alas! too soon outgrown;
Whilst a lonely stubborn Oak,
Which no Breezes can provoke,
No less Gusts persuade to move,
Than those, which in a Whirlwind drove,
Spoil'd the old Fraternal Feast,
And left alive but one poor Guest;
Rivell'd the distorted Trunk,
Sapless Limbs all bent, and shrunk,
Sadly does the Time presage,
Of our too near approaching Age.
When a helpless Vine is found,
Unsupported on the Ground,
Careless all the Branches spread,
Subject to each haughty Tread,
Bearing neither Leaves, nor Fruit,
Living only in the Root;
Back reflecting let me say,
So the sad Ardelia lay;
Blasted by a Storm of Fate,
Felt, thro' all the British State;
Fall'n, neglected, lost, forgot,
Dark Oblivion all her Lot;
Faded till Arminda's Love,

(Guided by the Pow'rs above)
Warm'd anew her drooping Heart,
And Life diffus'd thro' every Part;
Mixing Words, in wise Discourse,
Of such Weight and wond'rous Force,
As could all her Sorrows charm,
And transitory Ills disarm;
Chearing the delightful Day,
When dispos'd to be more Gay,
With Wit, from an unmeasured Store,
To Woman ne'er allow'd before.
What Nature, or refining Art,
All that Fortune cou'd impart,
Heaven did to Arminda send;
Then gave her for Ardelia's Friend:
To her Cares the Cordial drop,
Which else had overflow'd the Cup.
So, when once the Son of Jess,
Every Anguish did oppress,
Hunted by all kinds of Ills,
Like a Partridge on the Hills;
Trains were laid to catch his Life,
Baited with a Royal Wife,
From his House, and Country torn,
Made a Heathen Prince's Scorn;
Fate, to answer all these Harms,
Threw a Friend into his Arms.
Friendship still has been design'd,
The Support of Human-kind;
The safe Delight, the useful Bliss,
The next World's Happiness, and this.
Give then, O indulgent Fate!
Give a Friend in that Retreat
(Tho' withdrawn from all the rest)
Still a Clue, to reach my Breast.
Let a Friend be still convey'd
Thro' those Windings, and that Shade!

  Where, may I remain secure,
Waste, in humble Joys and pure,
A Life, that can no Envy yield;
Want of Affluence my Shield.
Thus, had Crassus been content,
When from Marius Rage he went,
With the Seat that Fortune gave,
The commodious ample Cave,
Form'd, in a divided Rock,
By some mighty Earthquake's Shock,

Into Rooms of every Size,
Fair, as Art cou'd e'er devise,
Leaving, in the marble Roof,
('Gainst all Storms and Tempests proof)
Only Passage for the Light,
To refresh the chearful Sight,
Whilst Three Sharers in his Fate,
On th' Escape with Joy dilate,
Beds of Moss their Bodies bore,
Canopy'd with Ivy o'er;
Rising Springs, that round them play'd,
O'er the native Pavement stray'd;
When the Hour arriv'd to Dine,
Various Meats, and sprightly Wine,
On some neighb'ring Cliff they spy'd;
Every Day a-new supply'd
By a Friend's entrusted Care;
Had He still continu'd there,
Made that lonely wond'rous Cave
Both his Palace, and his Grave;
Peace and Rest he might have found,
(Peace and Rest are under Ground)
Nor have been in that Retreat,
Fam'd for a Proverbial Fate;
In pursuit of Wealth been caught,
And punish'd with a golden Draught.
Nor had He, who Crowds cou'd blind,
Whisp'ring with a snowy Hind,
Made 'em think that from above,
(Like the great Imposter's Dove)
Tydings to his Ears she brought,
Rules by which he march'd and fought,
After Spain he had o'er-run,
Cities sack'd, and Battles won,
Drove Rome's Consuls from the Field,
Made her darling Pompey yield,
At a fatal, treacherous Feast,
Felt a Dagger in his Breast;
Had he his once-pleasing Thought
Of Solitude to Practice brought;
Had no wild Ambition sway'd;
In those Islands had he stay'd,
Justly call'd the Seats of Rest,
Truly Fortunate, and Blest,
By the ancient Poets giv'n
As their best discover'd Heav'n.
Let me then, indulgent Fate!
Let me still, in my Retreat,

From all roving Thoughts be freed,
Or Aims, that may Contention breed:
Nor be my Endeavours led
By Goods, that perish with the Dead!
Fitly might the Life of Man
Be indeed esteem'd a Span,
If the present Moment were
Of Delight his only Share;
If no other Joys he knew
Than what round about him grew:
But as those, who Stars wou'd trace
From a subterranean Place,
Through some Engine lift their Eyes
To the outward, glorious Skies;
So th' immortal Spirit may,
When descended to our Clay,
From a rightly govern'd Frame
View the Height, from whence she came;
To her Paradise be caught,
And things unutterable taught.
Given me then, in that Retreat,
Give me, O indulgent Fate!
For all Pleasures left behind,
Contemplations of the Mind.
Let the Fair, the Gay, the Vain
Courtship and Applause obtain;
Let th' Ambitious rule the Earth;
Let the giddy Fool have Mirth;
Give the Epicure his Dish,
Ev'ry one their sev'ral Wish;
Whilst my Transports I employ
On that more extensive Joy,
When all Heaven shall be survey'd
From those Windings and that Shade.

Jupiter and the Farmer

When Poets gave their God in Crete a Birth,
Then Jupiter held Traffick with the Earth,
And had a Farm to Lett: the Fine was high,
For much the Treas'ry wanted a Supply,
By Danae's wealthy Show'r exhausted quite, and dry.
But Merc'ry, who as Steward kept the Court,
So rack'd the Rent, that all who made Resort
Unsatisfy'd return'd, nor could agree
To use the Lands, or pay his secret Fee;

'Till one poor Clown (thought subt'ler than the rest,
Thro' various Projects rolling in his Breast)
Consents to take it, if at his Desire
All Weathers tow'rds his Harvest may conspire;
The Frost to kill the Worm, the brooding Snow,
The filling Rains may come, and Phoebus glow.
The Terms accepted, sign'd and seal'd the Lease,
His Neighbours Grounds afford their due Encrease
The Care of Heav'n; the Owner's Cares may cease.
Whilst the new Tenant, anxious in his Mind,
Now asks a Show'r, now craves a rustling Wind
To Raise what That had lodg'd, that he the Sheaves may bind.
The Sun, th'o'er-shadowing Clouds, the moistning Dews
He with such Contrariety does chuse;
So often and so oddly shifts the Scene,
Whilst others Load, he scarce has what to Glean.
  O Jupiter! with Famine pinch'd he cries,
No more will I direct th' unerring Skies;
No more my Substance on a Project lay,
No more a sullen Doubt I will betray,
Let me but live to Reap, do Thou appoint the way.

The Decision of Fortune

A FABLE

Fortune well-Pictur'd on a rolling Globe,
With waving Locks, and thin transparent Robe,
A Man beholding, to his Neighbor cry'd,
Whoe'er would catch this Dame, must swiftly ride.
Mark, how she seems to Fly, and with her bears,
All that is worth a busie Mortal's Cares:
The gilded Air about her Statue shines,
As if the Earth had lent it all her Mines;
At random Here a Diadem she flings,
And There a scarlet Hat with dangling Strings,
And to ten Thousand Fools ten Thousand glorious Things.
Shall I then stay at Home, Dull and Content
With Quarter-Days, and hard extorted Rent?
No, I'll to Horse, to Sea, to utmost Isles,
But I'll encounter her propitious Smiles:
Whilst you in slothful Ease may chuse to Sleep,
And scarce the few Paternal Acres keep.
Farewel, reply'd his Friend, may you advance,
And grow the Darling of this Lady Chance:
Whilst I indeed, not courting of her Grace,

Shall dwell content, in this my Native Place,
Hoping I still shall for your Friend be known:
But if too big for such Acquaintance grown,
I shan't be such a fond mistaken Sot,
To think Remembrance should become my Lot;
When you Exalted, have your self Forgot.
Nor me Ambitious ever shall you find,
Or hunting Fortune, who, they say, is Blind:
But if her Want of Sight shou'd make her Stray,
She shou'd be Welcome, if she came this way.
'Tis very like (the Undertaker cry'd)
That she her steps to these lost Paths shou'd guide:
But I lose Time, whilst I such Thoughts deride.
Away he goes, with Expectation chear'd,
But when his Course he round the World had steer'd,
And much had borne, and much had hop'd and fear'd,
Yet cou'd not be inform'd where he might find
This fickle Mistress of all Human-kind:
He quits at length the Chace of flying Game,
And back as to his Neighbor's House he came,
He there encounters the uncertain Dame;
Who lighting from her gaudy Coach in haste,
To him her eager Speeches thus addrest.
Fortune behold, who has been long pursu'd,
Whilst all the Men, that have my Splendors view'd,
Madly enamour'd, have such Flatt'ries forg'd,
And with such Lies their vain Pretensions urg'd,
That Hither I am fled to shun their Suits,
And by free Choice conclude their vain Disputes;
Whilst I the Owner of this Mansion bless,
And he unseeking Fortune shall possess.
Tho' rightly charg'd as something Dark of Sight,
Yet Merit, when 'tis found, is my Delight;
To Knaves and Fools, when I've some Grace allow'd,
'T has been like scattering Money in a Croud,
To make me Sport, as I beheld them strive,
And some observ'd (thro' Age) but Half-alive;
Scrambling amongst the Vigorous and Young,
One proves his Sword, and One his wheedling Tongue,
All striving to obtain me right or wrong;
Whilst Crowns, and Crosiers in the Contest hurl'd,
Shew'd me a Farce in the contending World.
Thou wert deluded, whilst with Ship, or Steed,
Thou lately didst attempt to reach my Speed,
And by laborious Toil, and endless Pains,
Didst sell thy Quiet for my doubtful Gains:
Whilst He alone my real Fav'rite rises,
Who every Thing to its just Value prizes,

And neither courts, nor yet my Gifts despises.

The Brass-Pot, and Stone-Jugg

A FABLE

A brazen Pot, by scouring vext,
With Beef and Pudding still perplext,
Resolv'd t' attempt a nobler Life,
Urging the Jugg to share the Strife:
Brother, quoth he, (Love to endear)
Why shou'd We Two continue here,
To serve and cook such homely Cheer?
Who tho' we move with awkward pace,
Your stony Bowels, and my Face,
Abroad can't miss of Wealth and Place.
Then let us instantly be going,
And see what in the World is Doing.
The bloated Jugg, supine and lazy,
Who made no Wish, but to be easy,
Nor, like it's Owner, e'er did think
Of ought, but to be fill'd with Drink;
Yet something mov'd by this fine Story,
And frothing higher with Vain-glory,
Reply'd, he never wanted Metal,
But had not Sides, like sturdy Kettle,
That in a Croud cou'd shove and bustle,
And to Preferment bear the Justle;
When the first Knock would break His Measures,
And stop his Rise to Place and Treasures.
Sure (quoth the Pot) thy Scull is thicker,
Than ever was thy muddiest Liquor:
Go I not with thee, for thy Guard,
To take off Blows, and Dangers ward?
And hast thou never heard, that Cully
Is borne thro' all by daring Bully?
Your self (reply'd the Drink-conveigher)
May be my Ruin and Betrayer:
A Superiority you boast,
And dress the Meat, I but the Toast:
Than mine your Constitution's stronger,
And in Fatigues can hold out longer;
And shou'd one Bang from you be taken,
I into Nothing shou'd be shaken.
A d'autre cry'd the Pot in scorn,
Dost think, there's such a Villain born,

That, when he proffers Aid and Shelter,
Will rudely fall to Helter-Skelter?
No more, but follow to the Road,
Where Each now drags his pond'rous Load,
And up the Hill were almost clamber'd,
When (may it ever be remember'd!)
Down rolls the Jugg, and after rattles
The most perfidious of all Kettles;
At every Molehill gives a Jump,
Nor rests, till by obdurate Thump,
The Pot of Stone, to shivers broken,
Sends each misguided Fool a Token:
To show them, by this fatal Test,
That Equal Company is best,
Where none Oppress, nor are Opprest.

Fanscomb Barn

In Imitation of MILTON

In Fanscomb Barn (who knows not Fanscomb Barn?)
Seated between the sides of rising Hills,
Whose airy Tops o'erlook the Gallick Seas,
Whilst, gentle Stower, thy Waters near them flow,
To beautify the Seats that crown thy Banks.
       —In this Retreat
Through Ages pass'd consign'd for Harbour meet,
And Place of sweet Repose to Wand'rers poor,
The weary Strolepedon felt that Ease,
Which many a dangerous Borough had deny'd
To him, and his Budgeta lov'd Compeer;
Nor Food was wanting to the happy Pair,
Who with meek Aspect, and precarious Tone,
Well suited to their Hunger and Degree,
Had mov'd the Hearts of hospitable Dames,
To furnish such Repast as Nature crav'd.
Whilst more to please the swarthy Bowl appears,
Replete with Liquor, globulous to fight,
And threat'ning Inundation o'er the Brim;
Yet, ere it to the longing Lips was rais'd
Of him who held it at its due Desert,
And more than all entreated Bounty priz'd,
Into the strong Profundity he throws
The floating Healths of Females, blith and young,
Who there had rendezvouz'd in past Delight,
And to stol'n Plenty added clamorous Mirth,

With Song and Dance, and every jovial Prank
Befitting buxom Crew, untied by Forms:
Whilst kind Budgeta nam'd such sturdy Youths,
As next into her tender Thoughts revolv'd,
And now were straggling East, and West, and South,
Hoof-beating, and at large, as Chance directs,
Still shifting Paths, lest Men (tho' stil'd of Peace)
Should urge their calmer Thoughts to Iron War,
Or force them to promote coercive Laws,
Beating that Hemp which oft entraps their Lives;
Or into Cordage pleated, and amass'd,
Deprives unruly Flesh of tempting Skin.
Thus kind Remembrance brought the Absent near
And hasten'd the Return of either's Pledge:
Brown were the Toasts, but not unsav'ry found
To Fancies clear'd by Exercise and Air,
Which the spirituous Nectar still improves,
And gliding now thro' every cherish'd Vein,
New Warmth diffus'd, new Cogitations bred,
With Self-conceit of Person, and of Parts.
When Strolepedon (late distorted Wight,
Limb-wanting to the View, and all mis-shap'd)
Permits a pinion'd Arm to fill the Sleeve,
Erst pendant, void, and waving with the Wind,
The Timber-Leg obsequiously withdraws,
And gives to that of Bone Precedence due.
Thus undisguis'd that Form again he wears,
Which Damsel fond had drawn from houshold Toils,
And strict Behests of Parents, old and scorn'd;
Whilst farther yet his Intellects confess
The bouzy Spell dilated and inhans'd,
Ripe for Description, and sett Turns of Speech,
Which to Conjugal Spouse were thus addrest.
My Wife (acknowledg'd such thro' maunding Tribes,
As long as mutual Love, the only Law,
Of Hedge or Barn, can bind our easy Faiths)
Be thou observant of thy Husband's Voice,
Sole Auditor of Flights and Figures bold;
Know, that the Valley which we hence descry
Richly adorn'd, is Fanscomb-Bottom call'd:
But whether from these Walls it takes the Name,
Or they from that, let Antiquaries tell,
And Men, well-read in Stories obsolete,
Whilst such Denomination either claims,
As speaks Affinity contiguous—
Thence let thy scatter'd Sight, and oft-griev'd Smell
Engulf the Sweets, and Colours free dispos'd
To Flowers promiscuous, and redundant Plants.

And (if the drouzy Vapour will admit,
Which from the Bowl soon triumphs o'er thy Lidds,
And Thee the weaker Vessel still denotes)
With Looks erect observe the verdant Slope
Of graceful Hills, fertile in Bush and Brake,
Whose Height attain'd, th' expatiated Downs
Shall wider Scenes display of rural Glee;
Where banner'd Lords, and fair escutcheon'd Knights,
With gentle Squires, and the Staff-griping Clown,
Pursue the trembling Prey impetuous;
Which yet escaping, when the Night returns,
And downy Beds enfold their careless Limbs,
More wakeful Trundle (Knapsack-bearing Cur)
Follows the Scent untrac'd by nobler Hounds,
And brings to us the Fruit of all their Toil.

　　Thus sung the Bard, whom potent Liquor rais'd,
Nor so contented, wish'd sublimer Aid.
Ye Wits! (he cry'd) ye Poets! (Loiterers vain,
Who like to us, in Idleness and Want
Consume fantastick Hours) hither repair,
And tell to list'ning Mendicants the Cause
Of Wonders, here observ'd but not discuss'd:
　Where, the White Sparrow never soil'd her Plumes,
　　Nor the dull Russet cloaths the Snowy Mouse.
To Helicon you might the Spring compare,
　That flows near Pickersdane renowned Stream,
Which, for Disport and Play, the Youths frequent,
Who, train'd in Learned School of ancient Wye,
First at this Fount suck in the Muses Lore,
When mixt with Product of the Indian Cane,
They drink delicious Draughts, and part inspir'd,
Fit for the Banks of Isis, or of Cham,
(For Cham, and Isis to the Bard were known,
A Servitor, when young in College-Hall,
Tho' vagrant Liberty he early chose,
Who yet, when Drunk, retain'd Poetick Phrase.)
Nor shou'd (quoth he) that Well, o'erhung with shade,
Amidst those neighb'ring Trees of dateless growth,
Be left unfathom'd by your nicer Skill
Who thence cou'd extricate a thousand Charms,
Or to oblivious Lethe might convert
The stagnant Waters of the sleepy Pool.
But most unhappy was that Morphean Sound
For lull'd Budgeta, who had long desir'd
Dismission fair from Tales, not throughly scann'd,
Thinking her Love a Sympathy confest,
When the Word Sleepy parted from his Lips,

Sunk affable and easy to that Rest,
Which Straw affords to Minds, unvex'd with Cares.

A Description of One of the Pieces of Tapistry at Long-Leat, made after the famous Cartons of Raphael;
in which, Elymas the Sorcerer is miraculously struck Blind by St. Paul before Sergius Paulus, the
Proconsul of Asia

Inscribed to the Honble Henry Thynne, under the Name of THEANOR

Thua Tapistry of old, the Walls adorn'd,
Ere noblest Dames the artful Shuttle scorn'd:
Arachne, then, with Pallas did contest,
And scarce th' Immortal Work was judg'd the Best.
Nor valorous Actions, then, in Books were fought;
But all the Fame, that from the Field was brought,
Employ'd the Loom, where the kind Consort wrought:
Whilst sharing in the Toil, she shar'd the Fame,
And with the Heroes mixt her interwoven Name.
No longer, Females to such Praise aspire,
And seldom now We rightly do admire.
So much, All Arts are by the Men engross'd,
And Our few Talents unimprov'd or cross'd;
Even I, who on this Subject wou'd compose,
Which the fam'd Urbin for his Pencil chose,
(And here, in tinctur'd Wool we now behold
Correctly follow'd in each Shade, and Fold)
Shou'd prudently from the Attempt withdraw,
But Inclination proves the stronger Law:
And tho' the Censures of the World pursue
These hardy Flights, whilst his Designs I view;
My burden'd Thoughts, which labour for a Vent,
Urge me t'explain in Verse, what by each Face is meant.
  Of SERGIUS first, upon his lofty Seat,
With due Regard our Observations treat;
Who, whilst he thence on ELYMAS looks down,
Contracts his pensive Brow into a Frown,
With Looks inquistive he seeks the Cause
Why Nature acts not still by Natures Laws.
'Twas but a Moment, since the Sorcerer's Sight
Receiv'd the Day, and blaz'd infernal Light:
Untouch'd, the Optiques in a Moment fail'd,
Their fierce Illumination quench'd, or veil'd;
Throughout th' Extention of his ample Sway,
No Fact, like this, the Roman cou'd survey,
Who, with spread Hands, invites Mankind to gaze,
And sympathize in the profound Amaze.

To share his Wonder every one combines,
By diff'rent Aspects shewn, and diff'rent Signs.
A comely Figure, near the Consul plac'd,
With serious Mildness and Instruction grac'd,
To Others seems imparting what he saw,
And shews the Wretch with reverential Awe:
Whilst a more eager Person next we find,
Viewing the Wizard with a Skeptic's Mind;
Who his fixt Eyes so near him do's apply,
We think, enliv'ning Beams might from them fly,
To re-inkindle, by so just an Aim,
The radial Sparks, but lately check'd and tame,
As Tapers new put-out will catch approaching Flame.
But dire Surprize th' Enquiry do's succeed,
Whilst full Conviction in his Face we read,
And He, who question'd, now deplores the Deed.
To sacred PAUL a younger Figure guides,
With seeming Warmth, which still in Youth presides;
And pointing forward, Elder Men directs,
In Him, to note the Cause of these Effects;
Upon whose Brow do's evidently shine
Deputed Pow'r, t' inflict the Wrath Divine;
Whilst sad and solemn, suited to their Years,
Each venerable Countenance appears,
Where, yet we see Astonishment reveal'd,
Tho' by the Aged often 'tis conceal'd;
Who the Emotions of their Souls disguize,
Lest by admiring they shou'd seem less Wise.
  But to thy Portrait, ELYMAS, we come
Whose Blindness almost strikes the Poet dumb;
And whilst She vainly to Describe thee seeks,
The Pen but traces, where the Pencil speaks.
Of Darkness to be felt, our Scriptures write,
Thou Darken'd seem'st, as thou would'st feel the Light;
And with projected Limbs, betray'st a Dread,
Of unseen Mischiefs, levell'd at thy Head.
Thro' all thy Frame such Stupefaction reigns,
As Night it self were sunk into thy Veins:
Nor by the Eyes alone thy Loss we find,
Each Lineament helps to proclaim thee Blind.
An artful Dimness far diffus'd we grant,
And failing seem all Parts through One important Want.
  Oh! Mighty RAPHAEL, justly sure renown'd!
Since in thy Works such Excellence is found;
No Wonder, if with Nature Thou'rt at strife,
Who thus can paint the Negatives of Life;
And Deprivation more expressive make,
Than the most perfect Draughts, which Others take.

Whilst to this Chiefest Figure of the Piece,
All that surround it, Heightnings do encrease:
In some, Amazement by Extreams is shewn,
Who viewing his clos'd Lids, extend their Own.
Nor can, by that, enough their Thoughts express,
Which op'ning Months seem ready to confess.
  Thus stand the LICTORS gazing on a Deed,
Which do's all humane Chastisements exceed;
Enfeebl'd seem their Instruments of smart,
When keener Words can swifter Ills impart.
  Thou, BARNABAS, though Last, not least our Care,
Seem'st equally employ'd in Praise, and Prayer,
Acknowledging th' Omnipotent Decree,
Yet soft Compassion in thy Face we see;
Whilst lifted Hands implore a kind Relief,
Tho' no Impatience animates thy Grief;
But mild Suspence and Charity benign,
Do all th' excesses of thy Looks confine.
  Thus far, our slow Imagination goes:
Wou'd the more skill'd THEANOR his disclose;
Expand the Scene, and open to our Sight
What to his nicer Judgement gives Delight;
Whose soaring Mind do's to Perfections climb,
Nor owns a Relish, but for Things sublime:
Then, wou'd the Piece fresh Beauties still present,
Nor Length of Time wou'd leave the Eye content:
As moments, Hours; as Hours the Days wou'd seem,
Observing here, taught to observe by HIM.

The Poor Man's Lamb:

OR,

Nathan's Parable to David after the Murder of Uriah, and his Marriage with Bathsheba

Turn'd into Verse and Paraphras'd

Now spent the alter'd King, in am'rous Cares,
The Hours of sacred Hymns and solemn Pray'rs:
In vain the Alter waits his slow returns,
Where unattended Incense faintly burns:
In vain the whisp'ring Priests their Fears express,
And of the Change a thousand Causes guess.
Heedless of all their Censures He retires,
And in his Palace feeds his secret Fires;
Impatient, till from Rabbah Tydings tell,

That near those Walls the poor Uriah fell,
Led to the Onset by a Chosen Few,
Who at the treacherous Signal, soon withdrew;
Nor to his Rescue e'er return'd again,
Till by fierce Ammon's Sword they saw the Victim slain.
'Tis pass'd, 'tis done! the holy Marriage-Knot,
Too strong to be unty'd, at last is cut.
And now to Bathsheba the King declares,
That with his Heart, the Kingdom too is hers;
That Israel's Throne, and longing Monarch's Arms
Are to be fill'd but with her widow'd Charms.
Nor must the Days of formal Tears exceed,
To cross the Living, and abuse the Dead.
This she denies; and signs of Grief are worn;
But mourns no more than may her Face adorn,
Give to those Eyes, which Love and Empire fir'd,
A melting Softness more to be desir'd;
Till the fixt Time, tho' hard to be endur'd,
Was pass'd, and a sad Consort's Name procur'd:
When, with the Pomp that suits a Prince's Thought,
By Passion sway'd, and glorious Woman taught,
A Queen she's made, than Michal seated higher,
Whilst light unusual Airs prophane the hallow'd Lyre.

Where art thou Nathan? where's that Spirit now,
Giv'n to brave Vice, tho' on a Prince's Brow?
In what low Cave, or on what Desert Coast,
Now Virtue wants it, is thy Presence lost?
But lo! he comes, the Rev'rend Bard appears,
Defil'd with Dust his awful silver Hairs,
And his rough Garment, wet with falling Tears.
The King this mark'd, and conscious wou'd have fled,
The healing Balm which for his Wounds was shed:
Till the more wary Priest the Serpents Art,
Join'd to the Dove-like Temper of his Heart,
And thus retards the Prince just ready now to part.
Hear me, the Cause betwixt two Neighbors hear,
Thou, who for Justice dost the Sceptre bear:
Help the Opprest, nor let me weep alone
For him, that calls for Succour from the Throne.
Good Princes for Protection are Ador'd,
And Greater by the Shield, than by the Sword.
This clears the Doubt, and now no more he fears
The Cause his Own, and therefore stays and hears:
When thus the Prophet: –
                    –In a flow'ry Plain
A King-like Man does in full Plenty reign;
Casts round his Eyes, in vain, to reach the Bound,

Which Jordan's Flood sets to his fertile Ground:
Countless his Flocks, whilst Lebanon contains
A Herd as large, kept by his numerous Swains,
That fill with morning Bellowings the cool Air,
And to the Cedar's shade at scorching Noon repair.
Near to this Wood a lowly Cottage stands,
Built by the humble Owner's painful Hands;
Fenc'd by a Stubble-roof, from Rain and Heat,
Secur'd without, within all Plain and Neat.
A Field of small Extent surrounds the Place,
In which One single Ewe did sport and graze:
This his whole Stock, till in full time there came,
To bless his utmost Hopes, a snowy Lamb;
Which, lest the Season yet too Cold might prove,
And Northern Blasts annoy it from the Grove,
Or tow'ring Fowl on the weak Prey might sieze,
(For with his Store his Fears must too increase)
He brings it Home, and lays it by his Side,
At once his Wealth, his Pleasure and his Pride;
Still bars the Door, by Labour call'd away,
And, when returning at the Close of Day,
With One small Mess himself, and that sustains,
And half his Dish it shares, and half his slender Gains.
When to the great Man's table now there comes
A Lord as great, follow'd by hungry Grooms:
For these must be provided sundry Meats,
The best for Some, for Others coarser Cates.
One Servant, diligent above the rest
To help his Master to contrive the Feast,
Extols the Lamb was nourished with such Care,
So fed, so lodg'd, it must be Princely Fare;
And having this, my Lord his own may spare.
In haste he sends, led by no Law, but Will,
Not to entreat, or purchase, but to Kill.
The Messenger's arriv'd: the harmless Spoil,
Unus'd to fly, runs Bleating to the Toil:
Whilst for the Innocent the Owner fear'd,
And, sure wou'd move, cou'd Poverty be heard.
Oh spare (he cries) the Product of my Cares,
My Stock's Encrease, the Blessing on my Pray'rs;
My growing Hope, and Treasure of my Life!
More was he speaking, when the murd'ring Knife
Shew'd him, his Suit, tho' just, must be deny'd,
And the white Fleece in its own Scarlet dy'd;
Whilst the poor helpless Wretch stands weeping by,
And lifts his Hands for Justice to the Sky.

Which he shall find, th' incensed King replies,

When for the proud Offence th' Oppressor dies.
O Nathan! by the Holy Name I swear,
Our Land such Wrongs unpunished shall not bear
If, with the Fault, th' Offender thou declare.

   To whom the Prophet, closing with the Time,
Thou art the Man replies, and thine th' ill-natur'd Crime.
Nor think, against thy Place, or State, I err;
A Pow'r above thee does this Charge prefer;
Urg'd by whose Spirit, hither am I brought
T' expostulate his Goodness and thy Fault;
To lead thee back to those forgotten Years,
In Labour spent, and lowly Rustick Cares,
When in the Wilderness thy Flocks but few,
Thou didst the Shepherd's simple Art pursue
Thro' crusting Frosts, and penetrating Dew:
Till wondring Jesse saw six Brothers past,
And Thou Elected, Thou the Least and Last;
A Sceptre to thy Rural Hand convey'd,
And in thy Bosom Royal Beauties laid;
A lovely Princess made thy Prize that Day,
When on the shaken Ground the Giant lay
Stupid in Death, beyond the Reach of Cries
That bore thy shouted Fame to list'ning Skies,
And drove the flying Foe as fast away,
As Winds, of old, Locusts to Egypt's Sea.
Thy Heart with Love, thy Temples with Renown,
Th' All-giving Hand of Heav'n did largely crown,
Whilst yet thy Cheek was spread with youthful Down.
What more cou'd craving Man of God implore?
Or what for favour'd Man cou'd God do more?
Yet cou'd not These, nor Israel's Throne, suffice
Intemp'rate Wishes, drawn thro' wand'ring Eyes.
One Beauty (not thy own) and seen by chance,
Melts down the Work of Grace with an alluring Glance;
Chafes the Spirit, fed by sacred Art,
And blots the Title AFTER GOD'S OWN HEART;
Black Murder breeds to level at his Head,
Who boasts so fair a Part'ner of his Bed,
Nor longer must possess those envy'd Charms,
The single Treasure of his House, and Arms:
Giving, by this thy Fall, cause to Blaspheme
To all the Heathen the Almighty Name.
For which the Sword shall still thy Race pursue,
And, in revolted Israel's scornful View,
Thy captiv'd Wives shall be in Triumph led
Unto a bold Usurper's shameful Bed;
Who from thy Bowels sprung shall seize thy Throne,

And scourge thee by a Sin beyond thy own.
Thou hast thy Fault in secret Darkness done;
But this the World shall see before the Noonday's Sun.
  Enough! the King, enough! the Saint replies,
And pours his swift Repentance from his Eyes;
Falls on the Ground, and tears the Nuptial Vest,
By which his Crime's Completion was exprest:
Then with a Sigh blasting to Carnal Love,
Drawn deep as Hell, and piercing Heaven, above
Let Me (he cries) let Me attend his Rod,
For I have sinn'd, for I have lost my God.
  Hold! (says the Prophet) of that Speech beware,
God ne'er was lost, unless by Man's Despair.
The Wound that is thus willingly reveal'd,
Th' Almighty is as willing should be heal'd.
Thus wash'd in Tears, thy Soul as fair does show
As the first Fleece, which on the Lamb does grow,
Or on the Mountain's top the lately fallen Snow.
Yet to the World that Justice may appear
Acting her Part impartial, and severe,
The Offspring of thy Sin shall soon resign
That Life, for which thou must not once repine;
But with submissive Grief his Fate deplore,
And bless the Hand, that does inflict no more.
  Shall I then pay but Part, and owe the Whole?
My Body's Fruit, for my offending Soul?
Shall I no more endure (the King demands)
And 'scape thus lightly his offended Hands?
Oh! let him All resume, my Crown, my Fame;
Reduce me to the Nothing, whence I came;
Call back his Favours, faster than he gave;
And, if but Pardon'd, strip me to my Grave:
  Since (tho' he seems to Lose) He surely Wins,
Who gives but earthly Comforts for his Sins.

Part of the Fifth Scene in the Second Act of Athalia, a Tragedy, written in French by Monsieur Racine

Enter, as in the Temple of Jerusalem, ATHALIA, MATHAN, ABNER.

Mathan
Why, to our Wonder, in this Place is seen,
Thus discompos'd, and alter'd, Juda's Queen?
May we demand, what Terrors seize your Breast,
Or, why your Steps are to this House addrest,
Where your unguarded Person stands expos'd
To secret Foes, within its Walls inclos'd?

Can it be thought that you remit that Hate?

Athalia
No more! but Both observe what I relate:
Not, that I mean (recalling Times of Blood)
To make you Judges of the Paths I trod,
When to the empty'd Throne I boldly rose,
Treating all Intercepters as my Foes.
'Twas Heav'ns Decree, that I should thus succeed,
Whose following Favour justifies the Deed,
Extending my unlimited Command
From Sea to Sea o'er the obedient Land:
Whilst your Jerusalem all Peace enjoys,
Nor now the' encroaching Philistine destroys,
Nor wandring Arab his Pavilion spreads,
Near Jordan's Banks, nor wastes his flow'ry Meads.
The great Assyrian, Terror of your Kings,
Who bought his Friendship with their holiest Things,
Yields that a Sister, of his pow'rful Race,
Should sway these Realms, and dignify the Place.
Nor need we add the late insulting Foe,
The furious Jehu does this Sceptre know,
And sinks beneath the Load of conscious Fears,
When in Samaria he my Actions hears.
Distrest by Foes, which I've against him rais'd,
He sees me unmolested, fix'd, and pleas'd;
At least, till now thus glorious was my State;
But something's threatned from relaxing Fate,
And the last Night, which should have brought me Rest,
Has all these great Ideas dispossest.
A Dream, a Vision, an apparent View
Of what, methinks, does still my Steps pursue,
Hangs on my pensive Heart, and bears it down
More than the weight of an objected Crown,
My Mother (be the Name with Rev'rence spoke!)
Ere chearful Day thro' horrid Shades had broke,
Approach'd my Bed, magnificent her Dress,
Her Shape, her Air did Jesabel confess:
Nor seem'd her Face to have refus'd that Art,
Which, in despight of Age, does Youth impart,
And which she practis'd, scorning to decay,
Or to be vanquish'd ev'n in Nature's way.
Thus all array'd, in such defying Pride
As when th' injurious Conqu'ror she descry'd,
And did in height of Pow'r for ill-got Pow'r deride.
To me she spake, these Accents to me came:
"Thou worthy Daughter of my soaring Fame,
"Tho' with a more transcendent Spirit fill'd,

"Tho' struggling Pow'rs attempt thy Life to shield,
"The Hebrew's God (Oh, tremble at the sound!)
"Shall Thee and Them, and all their Rights confound.
A pitying Groan concludes, no Word of Aid.
My Arms I thought to throw about the Shade
Of that lov'd Parent, but my troubled Sight
No more directed them to aim aright,
Nor ought presented, but a heap of Bones,
For which fierce Dogs contended on the Stones,
With Flakes of mangled Flesh, that quiv'ring still
Proclaim'd the Freshness of the suffer'd Ill;
Distain'd with Blood the Pavement, and the Wall,
Appear'd as in that memorable Fall—

Abner
Oh! just avenging Heaven!— [aside.

Mathan
Sure, Dreams like these are for Prevention given.

The SPLEEN

A Pindarick Poem

What art thou, SPLEEN, which ev'ry thing dost ape?
  Thou Proteus to abus'd Mankind,
  Who never yet thy real Cause cou'd find,
Or fix thee to remain in one continued Shape.
  Still varying thy perplexing Form,
  Now a Dead Sea thou'lt represent,
  A Calm of stupid Discontent,
Then, dashing on the Rocks wilt rage into a Storm.
  Trembling sometimes thou dost appear,
  Dissolv'd into a Panick Fear;
  On Sleep intruding dost thy Shadows spread,
  Thy gloomy Terrours round the silent Bed,
And croud with boading Dreams the Melancholy Head:
  Or, when the Midnight Hour is told,
And drooping Lids thou still dost waking hold,

  Thy fond Delusions cheat the Eyes,
  Before them antick Spectres dance,
Unusual Fires their pointed Heads advance,
  And airy Phantoms rise.
  Such was the monstrous Vision seen,
When Brutus (now beneath his Cares opprest,

And all Rome's Fortunes rolling in his Breast,
  Before Philippi's latest Field,
Before his Fate did to Octavius lead)
  Was vanquish'd by the Spleen.

  Falsly, the Mortal Part we blame
  Of our deprest, and pond'rous Frame,
  Which, till the First degrading Sin
  Let Thee, its dull Attendant, in,
  Still with the Other did comply,
Nor clogg'd the Active Soul, dispos'd to fly,
And range the Mansions of it's native Sky.

  Nor, whilst in his own Heaven he dwelt,
  Whilst Man his Paradice possest,
His fertile Garden in the fragrant East,
  And all united Odours smelt,
  No armed Sweets, until thy Reign,
  Cou'd shock the Sense, or in the Face
  A flusht, unhandsom Colour place.
Now the Jonquille o'ercomes the feeble Brain;
We faint beneath the Aromatick Pain,
Till some offensive Scent thy Pow'rs appease,
And Pleasure we resign for short, and nauseous Ease.

  In ev'ry One thou dost possess,
  New are thy Motions, and thy Dress:
  Now in some Grove a list'ning Friend
  Thy false Suggestions must attend,
Thy whisper'd Griefs, thy fancy'd Sorrows hear,
Breath'd in a Sigh, and witness'd by a Tear;

  Whilst in the light, and vulgar Croud,
  Thy Slaves, more clamorous and loud,
By Laughters unprovok'd, thy Influence too confess.
In the Imperious Wife thou Vapours art,
  Which from o'erheated Passions rise
  In Clouds to the attractive Brain,
  Until descending thence again,
  Thro' the o'er-cast, and show'ring Eyes,
  Upon her Husband's soften'd Heart,
  He the disputed Point must yield,
Something resign of the contested Field;
Til Lordly Man, born to Imperial Sway,
Compounds for Peace, to make that Right away,
And Woman, arm'd with Spleen, do's servilely Obey.

  The Fool, to imitate the Wits,

Complains of thy pretended Fits,
And Dulness, born with him, wou'd lay
Upon thy accidental Sway;
Because, sometimes, thou dost presume
Into the ablest Heads to come:
That, often, Men of Thoughts refin'd,
Impatient of unequal Sence,
Such slow Returns, where they so much dispense,
Retiring from the Croud, are to thy Shades inclin'd.
O'er me, alas! thou dost too much prevail:
I feel thy Force, whilst I against thee rail;
I feel my Verse decay, and my crampt Numbers fail.
Thro' thy black Jaundice I all Objects see,
As Dark, and Terrible as Thee,
My Lines decry'd, and my Employment thought
An useless Folly, or presumptuous Fault:
Whilst in the Muses Paths I stray,
Whilst in their Groves, and by their secret Springs
My Hand delights to trace unusual Things,
And deviates from the known, and common way;
Nor will in fading Silks compose
Faintly th' inimitable Rose,
Fill up an ill-drawn Bird, or paint on Glass
The Sov'reign's blurr'd and undistinguish'd Face,
The threatning Angel, and the speaking Ass.

Patron thou art to ev'ry gross Abuse,
The sullen Husband's feign'd Excuse,
When the ill Humour with his Wife he spends,
And bears recruited Wit, and Spirits to his Friends.
The Son of Bacchus pleads thy Pow'r,
As to the Glass he still repairs,
Pretends but to remove thy Cares,
Snatch from thy Shades one gay, and smiling Hour,
And drown thy Kingdom in a purple Show'r.
When the Coquette, whom ev'ry Fool admires,
Wou'd in Variety be Fair,
And, changing hastily the Scene
From Light, Impertinent, and Vain,
Assumes a soft, a melancholy Air,
And of her Eyes rebates the wand'ring Fires,
The careless Posture, and the Head reclin'd,
The thoughtful, and composed Face,
Proclaiming the withdrawn, the absent Mind,
Allows the Fop more liberty to gaze,
Who gently for the tender Cause inquires;
The Cause, indeed, is a Defect in Sense,
Yet is the Spleen alleg'd, and still the dull Pretence.

But these are thy fantastic Harms,
The Tricks of thy pernicious Stage,
Which do the weaker Sort engage;
Worse are the dire Effects of thy more pow'rful Charms.
By Thee Religion, all we know,
That shou'd enlighten here below,
Is veil'd in Darkness, and perplext
With anxious Doubts, with endless Scruples vext,
And some Restraint imply'd from each perverted Text.

Whilst Touch not, Taste not, what is freely giv'n,
Is but thy niggard Voice, disgracing bounteous Heav'n.
From Speech restrain'd, by thy Deceits abus'd,
To Desarts banish'd, or in Cells reclus'd,
Mistaken Vot'ries to the Pow'rs Divine,
Whilst they a purer Sacrifice design,
Do but the Spleen obey, and worship at thy Shrine.
In vain to chase thee ev'ry Art we try,
In vain all Remedies apply,
In vain the Indian Leaf infuse,
Or the parch'd Eastern Berry bruise;
Some pass, in vain, those Bounds, and nobler Liquors use.
Now Harmony, in vain, we bring,
Inspire the Flute, and touch the String.
From Harmony no help is had;
Musick but soothes thee, if too sweetly sad,
And if too light, but turns thee gayly Mad.

Tho' the Physicians greatest Gains,
Altho' his growing Wealth he sees
Daily increas'd by Ladies Fees,
Yet dost thou baffle all his studious Pains.
Not skilful Lower thy Source cou'd find,
Or thro' the well-dissected Body trace
The secret, the mysterious ways,
By which thou dost surprize, and prey upon the Mind.
Tho' in the Search, too deep for Humane Thought,
With unsuccessful Toil he wrought,
'Til thinking Thee to've catch'd, Himself by thee was caught,
Retain'd thy Pris'ner, thy acknowleg'd Slave,
And sunk beneath thy Chain to a lamented Grave.

An EPISTLE from Alexander to Hephæstion in His Sickness

With such a Pulse, with such disorder'd Veins,
Such lab'ring Breath, as thy Disease constrains;

With failing Eyes, that scarce the Light endure,
(So long unclos'd, they've watch'd thy doubtful Cure)
To his Hephæstion Alexander writes,
To soothe thy Days, and wing thy sleepless Nights,
I send thee Love: Oh! that I could impart,
As well my vital Spirits to thy Heart!
That, when the fierce Distemper thine wou'd quell,
They might renew the Fight, and the cold Foe repel
  As on Arbela's Plains we turn'd the Day,
When Persians through our Troops had mow'd their way,
When the rough Scythians on the Plunder run,
And barb'rous Shouts proclaim'd the Conquest won,
'Till o'er my Head (to stop the swift Despair)
The Bird of Jove fans the supporting Air,
Above my Plume does his broad Wings display,
And follows wheresoe'er I force my way:
Whilst Aristander, in his Robe of White,
Shews to the wav'ring Host th' auspicious Sight;
New Courage it inspires in ev'ry Breast,
And wins at once the Empire of the East.
Cou'd He, but now, some kind Presage afford,
That Health might be again to Thee restor'd;
Thou to my Wishes, to my fond Embrace;
Thy Looks the same, the same Majestick Grace,
That round thee shone, when we together went
To chear the Royal Captives in their Tent,
Where Sysigambis, prostrate on the Floor,
Did Alexander in thy Form adore;
Above great Æsculapius shou'd he stand,
Or made immortal by Apelles Hand.
But no reviving Hope his Art allows,
And such cold Damps invade my anxious Brows,
As, when in Cydnus plung'd, I dar'd the Flood
T' o'er-match the Boilings of my youthful Blood.
But Philip to my Aid repair'd in haste;
And whilst the proffer'd Draught I boldly taste,
As boldly He the dangerous Paper views,
Which of hid Treasons does his Fame accuse.
More thy Physician's Life on Thine depends,
And what he gives, his Own preserves, or ends.
If thou expir'st beneath his fruitless Care,
To Rhadamanthus shall the Wretch repair,
And give strict Answer for his Errors there.
  Near thy Pavilion list'ning Princes wait,
Seeking from thine to learn their Monarch's State.
Submitting Kings, that post from Day to Day,
To keep those Crowns, which at my Feet they lay,
Forget th' ambitious Subject of their Speed,

And here arriv'd, only Thy Dangers heed.
The Beauties of the Clime, now Thou'rt away,
Droop, and retire, as if their God of Day
No more upon their early Pray'rs would shine,
Or take their Incense, at his late Decline.
Thy Parisatis whom I fear to name,
Lest to thy Heat it add redoubl'd Flame;
Thy lovely Wife, thy Parisatis weeps,
And in her Grief a solemn Silence keeps.
Stretch'd in her Tent, upon the Floor she lies,
So pale her Looks, so motionless her Eyes,
As when they gave thee leave at first to gaze
Upon the Charms of her unguarded Face;
When the beauteous Sisters lowly knelt,
And su'd to those, who more than Pity felt.
To chear her now Statira vainly proves,
And at thy Name alone she sighs, and moves.
  But why these single Griefs shou'd I expose?
The World no Mirth, no War, no Bus'ness knows,
But, hush'd with Sorrow stands, to favour thy Repose.

Ev'n I my boasted Title now resign,
Not Ammon's Son, nor born of Race Divine,
But Mortal all, oppress'd with restless Fears,
Wild with my Cares, and Womanish in Tears.
Tho' Tears, before, I for lost Clytus shed,
And wept more Drops, than the old Hero bled;
Ev'n now, methinks, I see him on the Ground,
Now my dire Arms the wretched Corpse surround,
Now the fled Soul I wooe, now rave upon the Wound.
Yet He, for whom this mighty Grief did spring,
Not Alexander valu'd, but the King.
Then think, how much that Passion must transcend,
Which not a Subject raises but a Friend:
An equal Partner in the vanquished Earth,
A Brother, not impos'd upon my Birth,
Too weak a Tye unequal Thoughts to bind,
But by the gen'rous Motions of the Mind.

My Love to thee for Empire was the Test,
Since him, who from Mankind cou'd chuse the best,
The Gods thought only fit for Monarch o'er the rest.
Live then, my Friend; but if that must not be,
Nor Fate will with my boundless Mind agree,
Affording, at one time, the World and Thee;
To the most Worthy I'll that Sway resign,
And in Elysium keep Hyphæstion mine.

The following Lines Occasion'd by the Marriage of Edward Herbert Esquire, and Mrs. Elizabeth Herbert

Cupid one day ask'd his Mother,
  When she meant that he shou'd Wed?
You're too Young, my Boy, she said:
  Nor has Nature made another
  Fit to match with Cupid's Bed.

Cupid then her Sight directed
  To a lately Wedded Pair;
Where Himself the Match effected;
  They as Youthful, they as Fair.
Having by Example carry'd
  This first Point in the Dispute;
WORSELEY next he said's not Marry'd:
  Her's with Cupid's Charms may suit.

La Passion Vaincue

Done into ENGLISH with Liberty

On the Banks of the Severn a desperate Maid
  (Whom some Shepherd, neglecting his Vows, had betray'd,)
Stood resolving to banish all Sense of the Pain,
And pursue, thro' her Death, a Revenge on the Swain.
Since the Gods, and my Passion, at once he defies;
Since his Vanity lives, whilst my Character dies;
No more (did she say) will I trifle with Fate,
But commit to the Waves both my Love and my Hate.
And now to comply with that furious Desire,
Just ready to plunge, and alone to expire,
Some Reflection on Death, and its Terrors untry'd,
Some Scorn for the Shepherd, some Flashings of Pride
At length pull'd her back, and she cry'd, Why this Strife,
Since the Swains are so Many, and I've but One Life?

The Owl Describing her Young Ones

Why was that baleful Creature made,
Which seeks our Quiet to invade,
And screams ill Omens through the Shade?

'Twas, sure, for every Mortals good,
When, by wrong painting of her Brood,
She doom'd them for the Eagle's Food:

Who proffer'd Safety to her Tribe,
Wou'd she but shew them or describe,
And serving him, his Favour bribe.

When thus she did his Highness tell;
In Looks my Young do all excel,
Nor Nightingales can sing so well.

You'd joy to see the pretty Souls,
With wadling Steps and frowzy Poles,
Come creeping from their secret Holes.

But I ne'er let them take the Air,
The Fortune-hunters do so stare;
And Heiresses indeed they are.

This ancient Yew three hundred Years,
Has been possess'd by Lineal Heirs:
The Males extinct, now All is Theirs.

I hope I've done their Beauties right,
Whose Eyes outshine the Stars by Night;
Their Muffs and Tippets too are White.

The King of Cedars wav'd his Power,
And swore he'd fast ev'n from that Hour,
Ere he'd such Lady Birds devour.

Th' Agreement seal'd, on either part,
The Owl now promis'd, from her Heart,
All his Night-Dangers to divert;

As Centinel to stand and whoop,
If single Fowl, or Shoal, or Troop
Should at his Palace aim or stoop.

But home, one Evening without Meat,
The Eagle comes, and takes his Seat,
Where they did these Conditions treat.

The Mother-Owl was prol'd away,
To seek abroad for needful Prey,
And forth the Misses came to play.

What's here! the hungry Monarch cry'd,
When near him living Flesh he spy'd,
With which he hop'd to be supply'd.

But recollecting, 'twas the Place,
Where he'd so lately promis'd Grace
To an enchanting, beauteous Race;

He paus'd a while, and kept his Maw,
With sober Temperance, in awe,
Till all their Lineaments he saw.

What are these Things, and of what Sex,
At length he cry'd, with Vultur's Becks,
And Shoulders higher than their Necks?

These wear no Palatines, nor Muffs,
Italian Silks, or Doyley Stuffs,
But motley Callicoes, and Ruffs.

Nor Brightness in their Eyes is seen,
But through the Film a dusky Green,
And like old Margery is their Mien.

Then for my Supper they're design'd,
Nor can be of that lovely Kind,
To whom my Pity was inclin'd.

No more Delays; as soon as spoke,
The Plumes are stripped, the Grisles broke,
And near the Feeder was to choak.

When now return'd the grizly Dame,
(Whose Family was out of Frame)
Against League-Breakers does exclaim.

How! quoth the Lord of soaring Fowls,
(Whilst horribly she wails and howls)
Were then your Progeny but Owls?

I thought some Phoenix was their Sire,
Who did those charming Looks inspire,
That you'd prepar'd me to admire.

Upon your self the Blame be laid;
My Talons you've to Blood betray'd,
And ly'd in every Word you said.

Faces or Books, beyond their Worth extoll'd,
Are censur'd most, and thus to pieces pulled.

The Philosopher, the Young Man, and His Statue

A Fond Athenian Mother brought
A Sculptor to indulge her Thought,
  And carve her Only Son;
Who to such strange perfection wrought,
That every Eye the Statue caught
  Nor ought was left undone.
A youthful Smile adorn'd the Face,
The polish gave that Smile a Grace;
  And through the Marble reigns
(Which well the Artist's Skill cou'd trace,
And in their due Positions place)
  A Thread of purple Veins.

The Parasites about it came,
(Whose Praises were too large to name)
  And to each other said;
The Man so well had reach'd his Aim,
Th' Original cou'd o'er it claim
  Only a native Red.

Mean while a Sage, amidst the Croud,
Thus, with a Precept wise and loud,
  Check'd the Vain-glorious Boy;
By telling him, who now grew proud,
That tho' with Beauty 'twas endow'd,
  The Figure was a Toy:

Of no Advantage to the State,
'Twou'd neither combate, nor debate,
  But idly stand alone;
Bids him beware, whilst Men create
In Stone thus his Resemblance great,
  He proves not like the Stone.

The Hog, the Sheep, and Goat, Carrying to a FAIR

  Who does not wish, ever to judge aright,
    And, in the Course of Life's Affairs,
  To have a quick, and far extended Sight,

Tho' it too often multiplies his Cares?
And who has greater Sense, but greater Sorrow shares?

This felt the Swine, now carrying to the Knife;
   And whilst the Lamb and silent Goat
In the same fatal Cart lay void of Strife,
   He widely stretches his foreboding Throat,
Deaf'ning the easy Crew with his outragious Note.

The angry Driver chides th'unruly Beast,
   And bids him all this Noise forbear;
Nor be more loud, nor clamorous than the rest,
   Who with him travel'd to the neighb'ring Fair.
And quickly shou'd arrive, and be unfetter'd there.

This, quoth the Swine, I do believe, is true,
   And see we're very near the Town;
Whilst these poor Fools of short, and bounded View,
   Think 'twill be well, when you have set them down,
And eas'd One of her Milk, the Other of her Gown.

But all the dreadful Butchers in a Row,
   To my far-searching Thoughts appear,
Who know indeed, we to the Shambles go,
   Whilst I, whom none but Belzebub wou'd shear,
Nor but his Dam wou'd milk, must for my Carcase fear.

But tell me then, will it prevent thy Fate?
   The rude unpitying Farmer cries;
If not, the Wretch who tastes his Suff'rings late,
   Not He, who thro' th'unhappy Future prys,
Must of the Two be held most Fortunate and Wise.

The Shepherd and the Calm

Soothing his Passions with a warb'ling Sound,
A Shepherd-Swain lay stretch'd upon the Ground;
Whilst all were mov'd, who their Attention lent,
Or with the Harmony in Chorus went,
To something less than Joy, yet more than dull Content.
(Between which two Extreams true Pleasure lies,
O'er-run by Fools, unreach'd-at by the Wise)
But yet, a fatal Prospect to the Sea
Wou'd often draw his greedy Sight away.
He saw the Barques unlading on the Shore,
And guess'd their Wealth, then scorn'd his little Store.

Then wou'd that Little lose, or else wou'd make it more.
To Merchandize converted is the Fold,
The Bag, the Bottle, and the Hurdles sold;
The Dog was chang'd away, the pretty Skell
Whom he had fed, and taught, and lov'd so well.

In vain the Phillis wept, which heretofore
Receiv'd his Presents, and his Garlands wore.
False and upbraided, he forsakes the Downs,
Nor courts her Smiles, nor fears the Ocean's Frowns.
For smooth it lay, as if one single Wave
Made all the Sea, nor Winds that Sea cou'd heave;
Which blew no more than might his Sails supply:
Clear was the Air below, and Phoebus laugh'd on high.
With this Advent'rer ev'ry thing combines,
And Gold to Gold his happy Voyage joins;
But not so prosp'rous was the next Essay,
For rugged Blasts encounter'd on the way,
Scarce cou'd the Men escape, the Deep had all their Prey.
Our broken Merchant in the Wreck was thrown
Upon those Lands, which once had been his own;
Where other Flocks now pastur'd on the Grass,
And other Corydons had woo'd his Lass.

A Servant, for small Profits, there he turns,
Yet thrives again, and less and less he mourns;
Re-purchases in time th'abandon'd Sheep,
Which sad Experience taught him now to keep.
When from that very Bank, one Halcyon Day,
On which he lean'd, when tempted to the Sea,
He notes a Calm; the Winds and Waves were still,
And promis'd what the Winds nor Waves fulfill,
A settl'd Quiet, and Conveyance sure,
To him that Wealth, by Traffick, wou'd procure.
But the rough part the Shepherd now performs,
Reviles the Cheat, and at the Flatt'ry storms.
Ev'n thus (quoth he) you seem'd all Rest and Ease,
You sleeping Tempests, you untroubl'd Seas,
That ne'er to be forgot, that luckless Hour,
In which I put my Fortunes in your Pow'r;
Quitting my slender, but secure Estate,
My undisturb'd Repose, my sweet Retreat,
For Treasures which you ravish'd in a Day,
But swept my Folly, with my Goods, away.
Then smile no more, nor these false Shews employ,
Thou momentary Calm, thou fleeting Joy;
No more on me shall these fair Signs prevail,
Some other Novice may be won to Sail,

Give me a certain Fate in the obscurest Vale.

The LORD and the BRAMBLE

To view his stately Walks and Groves,
  A Man of Pow'r and Place
Was hast'ning on; but as he roves,
His Foe the slighted Bramble proves,
  And stops his eager Pace.

That Shrub was qualify'd to Bite;
  And now there went a Tale,
That this injurious partial Wight
Had bid his Gard'ner rid it quite,
  And throw it o'er the Pail.

Often the Bry'r had wish'd to speak,
  That this might not be done;
But from the Abject and the Weak,
Who no important Figure make,
  What Statesman does not run?

But clinging now about his Waste,
  Ere he had time to fly,
My Lord (quoth he) for all your haste,
I'll know why I must be displac'd,
  And 'mongst the Rubbish lie.

Must none but buffle-headed Trees
  Within your Ground be seen?
Or tap'ring Yews here court the Breeze,
That, like some Beaux whom Time does freeze,
  At once look Old and Green?

I snarl, 'tis true, and sometimes scratch
  A tender-footed Squire;
Who does a rugged Tartar catch,
When me he thinks to over-match,
  And jeers for my Attire.

As to Yourself, who 'gainst me fret,
  E'en give this Project o'er:
For know, where'er my Root is set,
These rambling Twigs will Passage get,
  And vex you more and more.

No Wants, no Threatnings, nor the Jail
  Will curb an angry Wit:
Then think not to chastise, or rail;
Appease the Man, if you'd prevail,
  Who some sharp Satire writ.

The CAUTIOUS LOVERS

Silvia, let's from the Croud retire;
  For, What to you and me
(Who but each other do desire)
  Is all that here we see?

Apart we'll live, tho' not alone;
  For, who alone can call
Those, who in Desarts live with One,
  If in that One they've All?

The World a vast Meander is,
  Where Hearts confus'dly stray;
Where Few do hit, whilst Thousands miss
  The happy mutual Way:

Where Hands are by stern Parents ty'd,
  Who oft, in Cupid's Scorn,
Do for the widow'd State provide,
  Before that Love is born:

Where some too soon themselves misplace;
  Then in Another find
The only Temper, Wit, or Face,
  That cou'd affect their Mind.

Others (but oh! avert that Fate!)
  A well-chose Object change:
Fly, Silvia, fly, ere 'tis too late;
  Fall'n Nature's prone to range.

And, tho' in heat of Love we swear
  More than perform we can;
No Goddess, You, but Woman are,
  And I no more than Man.

Th' impatient Silvia heard thus long;
  Then with a Smile reply'd;
Those Bands cou'd ne'er be very strong,

Which Accidents divide.

Who e'er was mov'd yet to go down,
  By such o'er-cautious Fear;
Or for one Lover left the Town,
  Who might have Numbers here?

Your Heart, 'tis true, Is worth them all,
  And still preferr'd the first;
But since confess'd so apt to fall,
  'Tis good to fear the worst.

In ancient History we meet
  A flying Nymph betray'd;
Who, had she kept in fruitful Crete,
  New Conquest might have made.

And sure, as on the Beach she stood,
  To view the parting Sails;
She curs'd her self, more than the Flood,
  Or the conspiring Gales.

False Theseus, since thy Vows are broke,
  May following Nymphs beware:
Methinks I hear how thus she spoke,
  And will not trust too far.

In Love, in Play, in Trade, in War
  They best themselves acquit,
Who, tho' their Int'rests shipwreckt are,
  Keep unreprov'd their Wit.

To DEATH

O King of Terrors, whose unbounded Sway
All that have Life, must certainly Obey;
The King, the Priest, the Prophet, all are Thine,
Nor wou'd ev'n God (in Flesh) thy Stroke decline.
My Name is on thy Roll, and sure I must
Encrease thy gloomy Kingdom in the Dust.
My soul at this no Apprehension feels,
But trembles at thy Swords, thy Racks, thy Wheels;
Thy scorching Fevers, which distract the Sense,
And snatch us raving, unprepar'd from hence;
At thy contagious Darts, that wound the Heads
Of weeping Friends, who wait at dying Beds.

Spare these, and let thy Time be when it will;
My Bus'ness is to Dye, and Thine to Kill.
Gently thy fatal Sceptre on me lay,
And take to thy cold Arms, insensibly, thy Prey.

ADAM Pos'd

Cou'd our First Father, at his toilsome Plough,
Thorns in his Path, and Labour on his Brow,
Cloath'd only in a rude, unpolish'd Skin,
Cou'd he a vain Fantastick Nymph have seen,
In all her Airs, in all her antick Graces,
Her various Fashions, and more various Faces;
How had it pos'd that Skill, which late assign'd
Just Appellations to Each several Kind!
A right Idea of the Sight to frame;
T'have guest from what New Element she came;
T'have hit the wav'ring Form, or giv'n this Thing a Name.

The House of Socrates

For Socrates a House was built,
  Of but inferiour Size;
Not highly Arch'd, nor Carv'd, nor Gilt;
  The Man, 'tis said, was Wise.
But Mob despis'd the little Cell,
  That struck them with no Fear;
Whilst Others thought, there should not dwell
  So great a Person there.

How shou'd a due Recourse be made
  To One, so much Admir'd?
Where shou'd the spacious Cloth be laid,
  Or where the Guests retir'd?

Believe me, quoth the list'ning Sage,
  'Twas not to save the Charge;
That in this over-building Age,
  My House was not more large.

But this for faithful Friends, and kind,
  Was only meant by me;
Who fear that what too streight you find,
  Must yet contracted be.

The EQUIPAGE

Written Originally in FRENCH by L'Abbé Reigner

Since the Road of Life's so ill;
I, to pass it, use this Skill,
My frail Carriage driving home
To its latest Stage, the Tomb.
Justice first, in Harness strong,
Marches stedfastly along:
Charity, to smooth the Pace,
Fills the next adjoining Trace:
Independance leads the Way,
Whom no heavy Curb do's sway;

Truth an equal Part sustains,
All indulg'd the loosen'd Reins:
In the Box fits vig'rous Health,
Shunning miry Paths of Wealth:
Gaiety with easy Smiles,
Ev'ry harsher Step beguiles;
Whilst of Nature, or of Fate
Only This I wou'd intreat:
The Equipage might not decay,
Till the worn Carriage drops away.

The Young RAT and his DAM, the COCK and the CAT

No Cautions of a Matron, Old and Sage,
Young Rattlehead to Prudence cou'd engage;
But forth the Offspring of her Bed wou'd go,
Nor reason gave, but that he wou'd do so.
Much Counsel was, at parting, thrown away,
Ev'n all, that Mother-Rat to Son cou'd say;
Who follow'd him with utmost reach of Sight,
Then, lost in Tears, and in abandon'd Plight,
Turn'd to her mournful Cell, and bid the World Good-Night.
But Fortune, kinder than her boding Thought,
In little time the Vagrant homewards brought,
Rais'd in his Mind, and mended in his Dress,
Who the Bel-air did every way confess,
Had learnt to flow'r his Wigg, nor brusht away
The falling Meal, that on his Shoulders lay;

And from a Nutshell, wimbl'd by a Worm,
Took Snuff, and cou'd the Government reform.
The Mother, weeping from Maternal Love,
To see him thus prodigiously improve,
Expected mighty Changes too, within,
And Wisdom to avoid the Cat, and Gin.
Whom did you chiefly note, Sweetheart, quoth she,
Of all the Strangers you abroad did see?
Who grac'd you most, or did your Fancy take?
The younger Rat than curs'd a noisy Rake,
That barr'd the best Acquaintance he cou'd make;
And fear'd him so, he trembl'd ev'ry Part;
Nor to describe him, scarce cou'd have the Heart.
High on his Feet (quoth he) himself he bore,
And terribly, in his own Language, swore;
A feather'd Arm came out from either Side,
Which loud he clapp'd, and Combatants defy'd,
And to each Leg a Bayonette was ty'd:
And certainly his Head with Wounds was sore;
For That, and both his Cheeks a Sanguine Colour wore.
Near Him there lay the Creature I admir'd,
And for a Friend by Sympathy desir'd:
His Make, like Ours, as far as Tail and Feet,
With Coat of Furr in parallel do meet;
Yet seeming of a more exalted Race,
Tho' humble Meekness beautify'd his Face:
A purring Sound compos'd his gentle Mind,
Whilst frequent Slumbers did his Eye-lids bind;
Whose soft, contracted Paw lay calmly still,
As if unus'd to prejudice, or kill.

I paus'd a while, to meditate a Speech,
And now was stepping just within his reach;
When that rude Clown began his hect'ring Cry,
And made me for my Life, and from th' Attempt to fly.
Indeed 'twas Time, the shiv'ring Beldam said,
To scour the Plain, and be of Life afraid.
Thou base, degen'rate Seed of injur'd Rats,
Thou veriest Fool (she cry'd) of all my Brats;
Would'st thou have shaken Hands with hostile Cats,
And dost not yet thine Own, and Country's Foe,
At this expence of Time, and Travel know?
Alas! that swearing, staring, bullying Thing,
That tore his Throat, and blustered with his Wing,
Was but some paltry, Dunghill, Craven Cock,
Who serves the early Household for a Clock.
And We his Oats, and Barley often steal,
Nor fear, he shou'd revenge the pilfer'd Meal:

Whilst that demure, and seeming harmless Puss
Herself, and mewing Chits regales with Us.
If then, of useful Sense thou'st gain'd no more,
Than ere thou'dst past the Threshold of my Door;
Be here, my Son, content to Dress and Dine,
Steeping the List of Beauties in thy Wine,
And neighb'ring Vermin with false Gloss outshine.

Amongst Mankind a Thousand Fops we see,
Who in their Rambles learn no more than Thee;
Cross o'er the Alpes, and make the Tour of France,
To learn a paltry Song, or antick Dance;
Bringing their Noddles, and Valizes pack'd
With Mysteries, from Shops and Taylors wreck'd:
But what may prejudice their Native Land;
Whose Troops are raising, or whose Fleet is mann'd,
Ne'er moves their Thoughts, nor do they understand.
Thou, my dear Rattlehead, and such as These
Might keep at home, and brood on Sloth and Ease:
Whilst Others, more adapted to the Age,
May vig'rously in Warlike Feats engage,
And live on foreign Spoils, or dying thin the Stage.

The Wit and the Beau

Strephon, whose Person ev'ry Grace
  Was careful to adorn;
Thought, by the Beauties of his Face,
In Silvia's Love to find a place,
  And wonder'd at her Scorn.
With Bows, and Smiles he did his Part;
  But Oh! 'twas all in vain:
A Youth less Fine, a Youth of Art
Had talk'd himself into her Heart,
  And wou'd not out again.

Strephon with change of Habits press'd,
  And urg'd her to admire;
His Love alone the Other dress'd,
As Verse, or Prose became it best,
  And mov'd her soft Desire.

This found, his courtship Strephon ends,
  Or makes it to his Glass;
There, in himself now seeks amends,
Convinc'd, that where a Wit pretends,

A Beau is but an Ass.

The EXECUTOR

A Greedy Heir long waited to fulfill,
As his Executor, a Kinsman's Will;
And to himself his Age repeated o'er,
To his Infirmities still adding more;
And nicely kept th' Account of the expected Store:
When Death, at last, to either gave Release,
Making One's Pains, the Other's Longings cease:
Who to the Grave must decently convey,
Ere he Possession takes the kindred Clay,
Which in a Coach was plac'd, wherein he rides,
And so no Hearse, or following Train provides;
Rejecting Russel, who wou'd make the Charge
Of one dull tedious Day, so vastly Large.
When, at his Death, the humble Man declar'd,
He wished thus privately to be Interr'd.
And now, the Luggage moves in solemn State,
And what it wants in Number, gains in Weight.
The happy Heir can scarce contain his Joy,
Whilst sundry Musings do his Thoughts employ,
How he shalt act, now Every thing's his Own,
Where his Revenge, or Favour shall be shown;
Then recollecting, draws a counterfeited Groan.
The Avenues, and Gardens shall be chang'd,
Already he the Furniture has ranged.
To ransack secret Draw'rs his Phancy flies,
Nor can th' appearing Wealth his Mind suffice.
Thus he an Age runs o'er betwixt the Porch
Of his Friend's House, and the adjacent Church:
Whilst the slow Driver, who no reck'ning kept
Of what was left, indulging Nature, slept;
Till on a Bank, so high, the Wheel was borne
That in a Moment All must overturn:
Whilst the rich Heir now finds the giving Dead
Less weighty in his Gold, than in his Lead;
Which falling just on his contriving Breast,
Expell'd the Soul, leaving the corpse to rest
In the same Grave, intended for his Friend.
Then why shou'd We our Days in Wishes spend,
Which, e'er we see fulfill'd, are often at an End?

Cupid and Folly

Imitated from the FRENCH

Cupid, ere depriv'd of Sight,
Young and apt for all Delight,
Met with Folly on the way,
As Idle and as fond of Play.
In gay Sports the time they pass;
Now run, now wrestle on the Grass;
Their painted Wings then nimbly ply,
And ev'ry way for Mast'ry try:
'Till a Contest do's arise,
Who has won th' appointed Prize.
Gentle Love refers the Case
To the next, that comes in Place;
Trusting to his flatt'ring Wiles,
And softens the Dispute with Smiles.
But Folly, who no Temper knows,
Words pursues with hotter Blows:
'Till the eyes of Love were lost,
Which has such Pain to Mortals cost.

Venus hears his mournful Crys,
And repeats 'em, in the Skys,
To Jupiter in Council set,
With Peers for the Occasion met;
In her Arms the Boy she bears,
Bathing him in falling Tears;
And whilst his want of Eyes is shown,
Secures the Judges by her Own.
Folly to the Board must come,
And hear the Tryal and the Doom;
Which Cytherea loudly prays
May be as heavy as the Case:
Which, when All was justly weigh'd,
Cupid's Wings now useless made,
That a staff, his Feet must guide,
Which wou'd still be apt to slide;
This Decree at last was read,
That Love by Folly shou'd be lead.

For the Better

Imitated from Sir Roger L'Estrange

A Quack, to no true Skill in Physick bred,
With frequent Visits cursed his Patient's Bed;
Enquiring, how he did his Broths digest,
How chim'd his Pulse, and how he took his Rest:
If shudd'ring Cold by Burnings was pursu'd,
And at what time the Aguish Fit renew'd.
The waining Wretch, each day become more faint,
In like proportion doubles his Complaint;
Now swooning Sweats he begs him to allay,
Now give his Lungs more liberty to play,
And take from empty'd Veins these scorching Heats away:
Or if he saw the Danger did increase,
To warn him fair, and let him part in Peace.
My Life for yours, no Hazard in your Case
The Quack replies; your Voice, your Pulse, your Face,
Good Signs afford, and what you seem to feel
Proceeds from Vapours, which we'll help with Steel.
With kindled Rage, more than Distemper, burns
The suff'ring Man, who thus in haste returns:
No more of Vapours, your belov'd Disease,
Your Ignorance's Skreen, your What-you-please,
With which you cheat poor Females of their Lives,
Whilst Men dispute not, so it rid their Wives.
For me, I'll speak free as I've paid my Fees;
My Flesh consumes, I perish by degrees:
And as thro' weary Nights I count my Pains,
No Rest is left me, and no Strength remains.
All for the Better, Sir, the Quack rejoins:
Exceeding promising are all these Signs.
Falling-away, your Nurses can confirm,
Was ne'er in Sickness thought a Mark of Harm.
The want of Strength is for the Better still;
Since Men of Vigour Fevers soonest kill.
Ev'n with this Gust of Passion I am pleas'd;
For they're most Patient who the most are seiz'd.

But let me see! here's that which all repels:
Then shakes, as he some formal Story tells,
The Treacle-water, mixt with powder'd Shells.
My Stomach's gone (what d'you infer from thence?)
Nor will with the least Sustenance dispense.
The Better; for, where appetite endures,
Meats intermingle, and no Med'cine cures.
The Stomach, you must know, Sir, is a Part—
But, sure, I feel Death's Pangs about my Heart.

  Nay then Farewel! I need no more attend
The Quack replies. A sad approaching Friend

Questions the Sick, why he retires so fast;
Who says, because of Fees I've paid the Last,
And, whilst all Symptoms tow'rd my Cure agree,
Am, for the Better, Dying as you see.

VERSES

Written under the King of Sweden's Picture

Observe this Piece, which to our Sight does bring
The fittest Posture for the Swedish King;
(Encompass'd, as we think, with Armies round,
Tho' not express'd within this narrow Bound)
Who, whilst his warlike and extended Hand
Directs the foremost Ranks to Charge or Stand,
Reverts his Face, lest That, so Fair and Young,
Should call in doubt the Orders of his Tongue:
Whilst the excited, and embolden'd Rear
Such Youth beholding, and such Features there,
Devote their plainer Forms, and are asham'd to Fear.
Thus! ev'ry Action, ev'ry Grace of thine,
O latest Son of Fame, Son of Gustavus Line!
Affects thy Troops, with all that can inspire
A blooming Sweetness, and a martial Fire,
Fatal to none, but thy invading Foe.
So Lightnings, which to all their Brightness shew,
Strike but the Man alone, who has provok'd the Blow.

A POEM for the Birth-Day of the Right Honble The Lady CATHARINE TUFTON

Occasion'd by sight of some Verses upon that Subject for the preceding Year, compos'd by no Eminent Hand

'Tis fit SERENA shou'd be sung.
High-born SERENA, Fair and Young,
Shou'd be of ev'ry Muse and Voice
The pleasing, and applauded Choice.
But as the Meanest of the Show
Do First in all Processions go:
So, let my Steps pursue that Swain
The humblest of th' inspired Train;
Whose well-meant Verse did just appear,
To lead on the preceding Year:
So let my Pen, the next in Fame,

Now wait on fair SERENA's Name;
The second Tribute gladly pay,
And hail this blest returning Day.
But let it not attempt to raise
Or rightly speak SERENA's Praise:
Since with more ease we might declare
How Great her Predecessors were;
How Great that more distinguish'd Peer,
To whom she owes her Being here;
In whom our Britain lets us see
What once they were, and still shou'd be;
As, when the earliest Race was drown'd,
Some Patterns, from amongst them found,
Were kept to shew succeeding Times
Their Excellence without their Crimes:
More easily we might express
What Vertues do her Mother dress;
What does her Form and Mind adorn,
Of whom th' engaging Nymph was born;
What Piety, what generous Love,
Does the enlarged Bosom move
Of Her, whose Fav'rite she appears,
Who more than as a Niece endears.
Such full Perfections obvious lie,
And strike, at first, a Poet's Eye.
Deep Lines of Honour all can hit,
Or mark out a superior Wit;
Consummate Goodness all can show,
And where such Graces shine below:
But the more tender Strokes to trace,
T' express the Promise of a Face,
When but the Dawnings of the Mind
We from the Air unripen'd find;
Which alt'ring, as new Moments rise,
The Pen or Pencil's Art defies;
When Flesh and Blood in Youth appears,
Polish'd like what our Marble wears;
Fresh as that Shade of op'ning Green,
Which first upon our Groves is seen;
Enliven'd by a harmless Fire,
And brighten'd by each gay Desire;
These nicer Touches wou'd demand
A Cowley's or a Waller's Hand,
T'explain, with undisputed Art,
What 'tis affects th'enlighten'd Heart,
When ev'ry darker Thought gives way,
Whilst blooming Beauty we survey;
To shew how All, that's soft and sweet,

Does in the fair SERENA meet;
To tell us, with a sure Presage,
The Charms of her maturer Age.
When Hothfeild shall (as heretofore
From its far-sought and virtuous Store
It Families of great Renown
Did with illustrious Hymens crown)
When Hothfeild shall such Treasure know,
As fair SERENA to bestow:
Then shou'd some Muse of loftier Wing
The Triumphs of that Season sing;
Describe the Pains, the Hopes, the Fears
Of noble Youths, th'ambitious Cares
Of Fathers, the long-fram'd Design,
To add such Splendour to their Line,
Whilst all shall strive for such a Bride
So Educated, and Ally'd.

A Tale of the Miser and the Poet

Written About the Year 1709

A wit, transported with Inditing,
Unpay'd, unprais'd, yet ever Writing;
Who, for all Fights and Fav'rite Friends,
Had Poems at his Fingers Ends;
For new Events was still providing;
Yet now desirous to be riding,
He pack'd-up ev'ry Ode and Ditty
And in Vacation left the City;
So rapt with Figures, and Allusions,
With secret Passions, sweet Confusions;
With Sentences from Plays well-known,
And thousand Couplets of his own;
That ev'n the chalky Road look'd gay,
And seem'd to him the Milky Way.
But Fortune, who the Ball is tossing,
And Poets ever will be crossing,
Misled the Steed, which ill he guided,
Where several gloomy Paths divided.
The steepest in Descent he follow'd,
Enclos'd by Rocks, which Time had hollow'd;
Till, he believ'd, alive and booted,
He'd reach'd the Shades by Homer quoted.
But all, that he cou'd there discover,
Was, in a Pit with Thorns grown over,

Old Mammon digging, straining, sweating,
As Bags of Gold he thence was getting;
Who, when reprov'd for such Dejections
By him, who liv'd on high Reflections,
Reply'd; Brave Sir, your Time is ended,
And Poetry no more befriended.
I hid this Coin, when Charles was swaying;
When all was Riot, Masking, Playing;
When witty Beggars were in fashion,
And Learning had o'er-run the Nation,
But, since Mankind is so much wiser,
That none is valued like the Miser,
I draw it hence, and now these Sums
In proper Soil grow up to Plumbs;
Which gather'd once, from that rich Minute
We rule the World, and all that's in it.

  But, quoth the Poet,can you raise,
As well as Plumb-trees, Groves of Bays?
Where you, which I wou'd chuse much rather,
May Fruits of Reputation gather?
Will Men of Quality, and Spirit,
Regard you for intrinsick Merit?
And seek you out, before your Betters,
For Conversation, Wit, and Letters?

  Fool, quoth the Churl, who knew no Breeding;
Have these been Times for such Proceeding?
Instead of Honour'd, and Rewarded,
Are you not Slighted, or Discarded?
What have you met with, but Disgraces?
Your PRIOR cou'd not keep in Places;
And your VAN-BRUG had found no Quarter,
But for his dabbling in the Morter.
ROWE no Advantages cou'd hit on,
Till Verse he left, to write North-Briton.
PHILIPS, who's by the Shilling known,
Ne'er saw a Shilling of his own.
Meets PHILOMELA, in the Town
Her due Proportion of Renown?
What Pref'rence has ARDELIA seen,
T'expel, tho' she cou'd write the Spleen?
Of Coach, or Tables, can you brag,
Or better Cloaths than Poet RAG?
Do wealthy Kindred, when they meet you,
With Kindness, or Distinction, greet you?
Or have your lately flatter'd Heroes
Enrich'd you like the Roman Maroes?

No–quoth the Man of broken Slumbers:
Yet we have Patrons for our Numbers;
There are Mecænas's among 'em.

Quoth Mammon,pray Sir, do not wrong 'em;
But in your Censures use a Conscience,
Nor charge Great Men with thriftless Nonsense:
Since they, as your own Poets sing,
Now grant no Worth in any thing
But so much Money as 'twill bring.
Then, never more from your Endeavours
Expect Preferment, or less Favours.
But if you'll 'scape Contempt, or worse,
Be sure, put Money in your Purse;
Money! which only can relieve you
When Fame and Friendship will deceive you.

Sir, (quoth the Poet humbly bowing,
And all that he had said allowing)
Behold me and my airy Fancies
Subdu'd, like Giants in Romances.
I here submit to your Discourses;
Which since Experience too enforces,
I, in that solitary Pit,
Your Gold withdrawn, will hide my Wit:
Till Time, which hastily advances,
And gives to all new Turns and Chances,
Again may bring it into use;
Roscommons may again produce;
New Augustean Days revive,
When Wit shall please, and Poets thrive.
Till when, let those converse in private,
Who taste what others don't arrive at;
Yielding that Mammonists surpass us;
And let the Bank out-swell Parnassus.

The CHANGE

Poor River, now thou'rt almost dry,
What Nymph, or Swain, will near thee lie?
Since brought, alas! to sad Decay,
What Flocks, or Herds, will near thee stay?
The Swans, that sought thee in thy Pride,
Now on new Streams forgetful ride:
And Fish, that in thy Bosom lay,

Chuse in more prosp'rous Floods to play.
All leave thee, now thy Ebb appears,
To waste thy sad Remains in Tears;
Nor will thy mournful Murmurs heed.
Fly, wretched Stream, with all thy speed,
Amongst those solid Rocks thy Griefs bestow;
For Friends, like those alas! thou ne'er did'st know.
  And thou, poor Sun! that sat'st on high;
But late, the Splendour of the Sky;
What Flow'r, tho' by thy Influence born,
Now Clouds prevail, will tow'rds thee turn?
Now Darkness sits upon thy Brow,
What Persian Votary will bow?
What River will her Smiles reflect,
Now that no Beams thou can'st direct?
By watry Vapours overcast,
Who thinks upon thy Glories past?
If present Light, nor Heat we get,
Unheeded thou may'st rise, and set.
Not all the past can one Adorer keep,
Fall, wretched Sun, to the more faithful Deep.
  Nor do thou, lofty Structure! boast,
Since undermin'd by Time and Frost:
Since thou canst no Reception give,
In untrod Meadows thou may'st live.
None from his ready Road will turn,
With thee thy wretched Change to mourn.
Not the soft Nights, or chearful Days
Thou hast bestow'd, can give thee Praise.
No lusty Tree that near thee grows,
(Tho' it beneath thy Shelter rose)
Will to thy Age a Staff become.
Fall, wretched Building! to thy Tomb.
Thou, and thy painted Roofs, in Ruin mixt,
Fall to the Earth, for That alone is fixt.
  The same, poor Man, the same must be
Thy Fate, now Fortune frowns on thee.
Her Favour ev'ry one pursues,
And losing Her, thou all must lose.
No Love, sown in thy prosp'rous Days,
Can Fruit in this cold Season raise:
No Benefit, by thee conferr'd,
Can in this time of Storms be heard.
All from thy troubl'd Waters run;
Thy stooping Fabrick all Men shun.
All do thy clouded Looks decline,
As if thou ne'er did'st on them shine.
O wretched Man! to other World's repair;

For Faith and Gratitude are only there.

Enquiry after Peace

A Fragment

Peace! where art thou to be found?
Where, in all the spacious Round,
May thy Footsteps be pursu'd?
Where may thy calm Seats be view'd?
On some Mountain dost thou lie,
Serenely near the ambient Sky,
Smiling at the Clouds below,
Where rough Storms and Tempests grow?
Or, in some retired Plain,
Undisturb'd dost thou remain?
Where no angry Whirlwinds pass,
Where no Floods oppress the Grass.

High above, or deep below,
Fain I thy Retreat wou'd know.
Fain I thee alone wou'd find,
Balm to my o'er-weary'd Mind.
Since what here the World enjoys,
Or our Passions most employs,
Peace opposes, or destroys.
Pleasure's a tumultuous thing,
Busy still, and still on Wing;
Flying swift, from place to place,
Darting from each beauteous Face;
From each strongly mingled Bowl
Through th'inflam'd and restless Soul.
Sov'reign Pow'r who fondly craves,
But himself to Pomp enslaves;
Stands the Envy of Mankind,
Peace, in vain, attempts to find.
Thirst of Wealth no Quiet knows,
But near the Death-bed fiercer grows;
Wounding Men with secret Stings,
For Evils it on Others brings.
War who not discreetly shuns,
Thorough Life the Gauntlet runs.
Swords, and Pikes, and Waves, and Flames,
Each their Stroke against him aims.
Love (if such a thing there be)
Is all Despair, or Extasie.

Poetry's the feav'rish Fit,
Th' o'erflowing of unbounded Wit. &c.

On the Death of the Honourable Mr. James Thynne, Younger Son to the Right Honourable the Lord Viscount Weymouth

Farewel, lov'd Youth! since 'twas the Will of Heaven
So soon to take, what had so late been giv'n;
And thus our Expectations to destroy,
Raising a Grief, where we had form'd a Joy;
Who once believ'd, it was the Fates Design
In Him to double an Illustrious Line,
And in a second Channel spread that Race
Where ev'ry Virtue shines, with every Grace.
But we mistook, and 'twas not here below
That this engrafted Scion was to grow;
The Seats above requir'd him, that each Sphere
Might soon the Offspring of such Parents share.
Resign him then to the supream Intent,
You, who but Flesh to that blest Spirit lent.
Again disrob'd, let him to Bliss retire,
And only bear from you, amidst that Choir,
What, Precept or Example did inspire,
A Title to Rewards, from that rich store
Of Pious Works, which you have sent before.
Then lay the fading Reliques, which remain,
In the still Vault (excluding farther Pain);
Where Kings and Counsellors their Progress close,
And his renowned Ancestors repose;

Where COVENTRY withdrew All but in Name,
Leaving the World his Benefits and Fame;
Where his Paternal Predecessor lies,
Once large of Thought, and rank'd among the Wise;
Whose Genius in Long-Leat we may behold
(A Pile, as noble as if he'd been told
By WEYMOUTH, it shou'd be in time possest,
And strove to suit the Mansion to the Guest.)
Nor favour'd, nor disgrac'd, there ESSEX sleeps,
Nor SOMERSET his Master's Sorrows weeps,
Who to the shelter of th' unenvy'd Grave
Convey'd the Monarch, whom he cou'd not save;
Though, Roman-like, his own less-valu'd Head
He proffer'd in that injur'd Martyr's stead.
Nor let that matchless Female 'scape my Pen,
Who their Whole Duty taught to weaker Men,

And of each Sex the Two best Gifts enjoy'd,
The Skill to write, the Modesty to hide;
Whilst none shou'd that Performance disbelieve,
Who led the Life, might the Directions give.
With such as These, whence He deriv'd his Blood,
Great on Record, or eminently Good,
Let Him be laid, till Death's long Night shall cease,
And breaking Glory interrupt the Peace.
Mean-while, ye living Parents, ease your Grief
By Tears, allow'd as Nature's due Relief.
For when we offer to the Pow'rs above,
Like You, the dearest Objects of our Love;
When, with that patient Saint in Holy Writ,
We've learnt at once to Grieve, and to Submit;
When contrite Sighs, like hallow'd Incense, rise
Bearing our Anguish to th' appeased Skies;
Then may those Show'rs, which take from Sorrow birth,
And still are tending tow'rd this baleful Earth,
O'er all our deep and parching Cares diffuse,
Like Eden's Springs, or Hermon's soft'ning Dews.
But lend your Succours, ye Almighty Pow'rs,
For as the Wound, the Balsam too is Yours.
In vain are Numbers, or persuasive Speech,
What Poets write, or what the Pastors teach,
Till You, who make, again repair the Breach.
For when to Shades of Death our Joys are fled,
When for a Loss, like This, our Tears are shed,
None can revive the Heart, but who can raise the Dead.
But yet, my Muse, if thou hadst softer Verse
Than e'er bewail'd the melancholy Herse;
If thou hadst Pow'r to dissipate the Gloom
Inherent to the Solitary Tomb;
To rescue thence the Memory and Air
Of what we lately saw so Fresh, so Fair;
Then shou'd this Noble Youth thy Art engage
To shew the Beauties of his blooming Age,
The pleasing Light, that from his Eyes was cast,
Like hasty Beams, too Vigorous to last;
Where the warm Soul, as on the Confines, lay
Ready for Flight, and for Eternal Day.
Gently dispos'd his Nature shou'd be shown,
And all the Mother's Sweetness made his Own.
The Father's Likeness was but faintly seen,
As ripen'd Fruits are figur'd by the Green.
Nor cou'd we hope, had he fulfill'd his Days,
He shou'd have reach'd WEYMOUTH's unequal'd Praise.
Still One distinguish'd plant each Lineage shews,
And all the rest beneath it's Stature grows.

Of Tully's Race but He possess'd the Tongue,
And none like Julius from the Caesars sprung.
Next, in his harmless Sports he shou'd be drawn
Urging his Courser, o'er the flow'ry Lawn;
Sprightly Himself, as the enliven'd Game,
Bold in the Chace, and full of gen'rous Flame;
Yet in the Palace, Tractable and Mild,
Perfect in all the Duties of a Child;
Which fond Reflection pleases, whilst it pains,
Like penetrating Notes of sad Harmonious Strains.
Selected Friendships timely he began,
And siezed in Youth that best Delight of Man,
Leaving a growing Race to mourn his End,
Their earliest and their Ages promis'd Friend.
But far away alas! that Prospect moves,
Lost in the Clouds, like distant Hills and Groves,
Whilst with encreasing Steps we all pursue
What Time alone can bring to nearer View,
That Future State, which Darkness yet involves,
Known but by Death, which ev'ry Doubt resolves.

The Critick and the Writer of FABLES

Weary, at last, of the Pindarick way,
Thro' which advent'rously the Muse wou'd stray;
To Fable I descend with soft Delight,
Pleas'd to Translate, or easily Endite:
Whilst aery Fictions hastily repair
To fill my Page, and rid my Thoughts of Care,
As they to Birds and Beasts new Gifts impart,
And Teach, as Poets shou'd, whilst they Divert.

But here, the Critick bids me check this Vein.
Fable, he crys, tho' grown th' affected Strain,
But dies, as it was born, without Regard or Pain.
Whilst of his Aim the lazy Trifler fails,
Who seeks to purchase Fame by childish Tales.

Then, let my Verse, once more attempt the Skies,
The easily persuaded Poet cries,
Since meaner Works you Men of Taste despise.
The Walls of Troy shall be our loftier Stage,
Our mighty Theme the fierce Achilles Rage.
The Strength of Hector, and Ulysses Arts
Shall boast such Language, to adorn their Parts,
As neither Hobbes, nor Chapman cou'd bestow,

Or did from Congreve, or from Dryden flow.
Amidst her Towers, the dedicated Horse
Shall be receiv'd, big with destructive Force;
Till Men shall say, when Flames have brought her down.
"Troy is no more, and Ilium was a Town.

Is this the way to please the Men of Taste,
The Interrupter cries, this old Bombast?
I'm sick of Troy, and in as great a Fright,
When some dull Pedant wou'd her Wars recite,
As was soft Paris, when compell'd to Fight.
To Shades and Springs shall we awhile repair,
The Muse demands, and in that milder Air
Describe some gentle Swain's unhappy Smart
Whose folded Arms still press upon his Heart,
And deeper drive the too far enter'd Dart?
Whilst Phillis with a careless pleasure reigns
The Joy, the Grief, the Envy of the Plains;
Heightens the Beauty of the verdant Woods,
And softens all the Murmurs of the Floods.

Oh! stun me not with these insipid Dreams,
Th' Eternal Hush, the Lullaby of Streams.
Which still, he cries, their even Measures keep,
Till both the Writers, and the Readers sleep.
But urge thy Pen, if thou wouldst move our Thoughts,
To shew us private, or the publick Faults.
Display the Times, High-Church or Low provoke;
We'll praise the Weapon, as we like the Stroke,
And warmly sympathizing with the Spite
Apply to Thousands, what of One you write.

Then, must that single Stream the Town supply,
The harmless Fable-writer do's reply,
And all the Rest of Helicon be dry?
And when so many choice Productions swarm,
Must only Satire keep your Fancies warm?
Whilst even there, you praise with such Reserve,
As if you'd in the midst of Plenty starve,
Tho' ne'er so liberally we Authors carve.

Happy the Men, whom we divert with Ease,
Whom Opera's and Panegyricks please.

Through ev'ry Age some Tyrant Passion reigns:
Now Love prevails, and now Ambition gains
Reason's lost Throne, and sov'reign Rule maintains.
Tho' beyond Love's, Ambition's Empire goes;
For who feels Love, Ambition also knows,
And proudly still aspires to be possest
Of Her, he thinks superior to the rest.
As cou'd be prov'd, but that our plainer Task
Do's no such Toil, or Definitions ask;
But to be so rehears'd, as first 'twas told,
When such old Stories pleas'd in Days of old.

  A King, observing how a Shepherd's Skill
Improv'd his Flocks, and did the Pastures fill,
That equal Care th' assaulted did defend,
And the secur'd and grazing Part attend,
Approves the Conduct, and from Sheep and Curs
Transfers the Sway, and changed his Wool to Furrs.
Lord-Keeper now, as rightly he divides
His just Decrees, and speedily decides;
When his sole Neighbor, whilst he watch'd the Fold,
A Hermit poor, in Contemplation old,
Hastes to his Ear, with safe, but lost Advice,
Tells him such Heights are levell'd in a trice,
Preferments treach'rous, and her Paths of Ice:
And that already sure 't had turn'd his Brain,
Who thought a Prince's Favour to retain.
Nor seem'd unlike, in this mistaken Rank,
The sightless Wretch, who froze upon a Bank
A Serpent found, which for a Staff he took,
And us'd as such (his own but lately broke)
Thanking the Fates, who thus his Loss supply'd,
Nor marking one, that with amazement cry'd,
Throw quickly from thy Hand that sleeping Ill;
A Serpent 'tis, that when awak'd will kill.
A Serpent this! th' uncaution'd Fool replies:
A Staff it feels, nor shall my want of Eyes
Make me believe, I have no Senses left,
And thro' thy Malice be of this bereft;
Which Fortune to my Hand has kindly sent
To guide my Steps, and stumbling to prevent.
No Staff, the Man proceeds; but to thy harm
A Snake 'twill prove: The Viper, now grown warm
Confirm'd it soon, and fasten'd on his Arm.

  Thus wilt thou find, Shepherd believe it true,

Some Ill, that shall this seeming Good ensue;
Thousand Distastes, t' allay thy envy'd Gains,
Unthought of, on the parcimonious Plains.
So prov'd the Event, and Whisp'rers now defame
The candid Judge, and his Proceedings blame.
By Wrongs, they say, a Palace he erects,
The Good oppresses, and the Bad protects.
To view this Seat the King himself prepares,
Where no Magnificence or Pomp appears,
But Moderation, free from each Extream,
Whilst Moderation is the Builder's Theme.
Asham'd yet still the Sycophants persist,
That Wealth he had conceal'd within a Chest,
Which but attended some convenient Day,
To face the Sun, and brighter Beams display.
The Chest unbarr'd, no radiant Gems they find,
No secret Sums to foreign Banks design'd,
But humble Marks of an obscure Recess,
Emblems of Care, and Instruments of Peace;
The Hook, the Scrip, and for unblam'd Delight
The merry Bagpipe, which, ere fall of Night,
Cou'd sympathizing Birds to tuneful Notes invite.
Welcome ye Monuments of former Joys!
Welcome! to bless again your Master's Eyes,
And draw from Courts, th' instructed Shepherd cries.
No more dear Relicks! we no more will part,
You shall my Hands employ, who now revive my Heart.
No Emulations, nor corrupted Times
Shall falsely blacken, or seduce to Crimes
Him, whom your honest Industry can please,
Who on the barren Down can sing from inward Ease.

   How's this! the Monarch something mov'd rejoins.
With such low Thoughts, and Freedom from Designs,
What made thee leave a Life so fondly priz'd,
To be in Crouds, or envy'd, or despis'd?

   Forgive me, Sir, and Humane Frailty see,
The Swain replies, in my past State and Me;
All peaceful that, to which I vow return.
But who alas! (tho' mine at length I mourn)
Was e'er without the Curse of some Ambition born.

An EPISTLE from a Gentleman to Madam Deshouliers, returning Money she had lent him at Bassette, upon the first Day of their Acquaintance

URANIA, whom the Town admires,
  Whose Wit and Beauty share our Praise;
This fair URANIA who inspires
  A thousand Joys a thousand ways,
She, who cou'd with a Glance convey
  Favours, that had my Hopes outdone,
Has lent me Money on that Day,
  Which our Acquaintance first begun.

Nor with the Happiness I taste,
  Let any jealous Doubts contend:
Her Friendship is secure to last,
  Beginning where all others end.
And thou, known Cheat! upheld by Law,
  Thou Disappointer of the craving Mind,
BASSETTE, who thy Original dost draw
  From Venice (by uncertain Seas confin'd);
Author of Murmurs, and of Care,
  Of pleasing Hopes, concluding in Despair:
To thee my strange Felicity I owe,
  From thy Oppression did this Succour flow.
Less had I gained, had'st thou propitious been,
  Who better by my Loss hast taught me how to Win.
Yet tell me, my transported Brain!
  (whose Pride this Benefit awakes)
Know'st thou, what on this Chance depends?
  And are we not exalted thus in vain,
Whilst we observe the Money which she lends,
  But not, alas! the Heart she takes,
The fond Engagements, and the Ties
  Her fatal Bounty does impose,
Who makes Reprisals, with her Eyes,
  For what her gen'rous Hand bestows?
And tho' I quickly can return
  Those useful Pieces, which she gave;
Can I again, or wou'd I have
  That which her Charms have from me borne?
Yet let us quit th' obliging Score;
And whilst we borrow'd Gold restore,
Whilst readily we own the Debt,
And Gratitude before her set
  In its approved and fairest Light;
Let her effectually be taught
  By that instructive, harmless Slight,
That also in her turn she ought
  (Repaying ev'ry tender Thought)

Kindness with Kindness to requite.

To Edward Jenkinson, Esq; a very young Gentleman, who writ a Poem on PEACE

Fair Youth! who wish the Wars may cease,
We own you better form'd for Peace.
Nor Pallas you, nor Mars shou'd follow;
Your Gods are Cupid and Apollo;
Who give sweet Looks, and early Rhimes,
Bespeaking Joys, and Halcyon Times.
Your Face, which We, as yet, may praise,
Calls for the Myrtle, and the Bays.
The Martial Crowns Fatigues demand,
And laurell'd Heroes must be tann'd;
A Fate, we never can allow
Shou'd reach your pleasing, polish'd Brow.
But granting what so young you've writ,
From Nature flow'd, as well as Wit;
And that indeed you Peace pursue,
We must begin to Treat with you.

We Females, Sir, it is I mean:
Whilst I, like BRISTOL for the QUEEN,
For all the Ladies of your Age
As Plenipo' betimes engage;
And as first Article declare,
You shall be Faithful as you're Fair:
No Sighs, when you shall know their Use,
Shall be discharg'd in Love's Abuse;
Nor kindling Words shall undermine,
Till you in equal Passion join.
Nor Money be alone your Aim,
Tho' you an Over-weight may claim,
And fairly build on your Desert,
If with your Person goes your Heart.
But when this Barrier I have gain'd,
And trust it will be well maintain'd;
Who knows, but some imprudent She
Betraying what's secur'd by me,
Shall yield thro' Verse, or stronger Charms,
To Treat anew on easier Terms?
And I be negligently told—
You was too Young, and I too Old,
To have our distant Maxims hold.

To the Painter of an ill-drawn Picture of CLEONE, the Honourable Mrs. Thynne

Sooner I'd praise a Cloud which Light beguiles,
Than thy rash Hand which robs this Face of Smiles;
And does that sweet and pleasing Air controul,
Which to us paints the fair CLEONE's Soul.
'Tis vain to boast of Rules or labour'd Art;
I miss the Look that captivates my Heart,
Attracts my Love, and tender Thoughts inspires;
Nor can my Breast be warm'd by common Fires;
Nor can ARDELIA love but where she first admires.
Like Jupiter's, thy Head was sure in Pain
When this Virago struggl'd in thy Brain;
And strange it is, thou hast not made her wield
A mortal Dart, or penetrating Shield,
Giving that Hand of disproportion'd size
The Pow'r, of which thou hast disarm'd her Eyes:
As if, like Amazons, she must oppose,
And into Lovers force her vanquish'd Foes.
Had to THEANOR thus her Form been shown
To gain her Heart, he had not lost his own;
Nor, by the gentlest Bands of Human Life,
At once secur'd the Mistress and the Wife.
For still CLEONE's Beauties are the same,
And what first lighten'd, still upholds his Flame.
Fain his Compassion wou'd thy Works approve,
Were pitying thee consistent with his Love,
Or with the Taste which Italy has wrought
In his refin'd and daily heighten'd Thought,
Where Poetry, or Painting find no place,
Unless perform'd with a superior Grace.
Cou'd but my Wish some Influence infuse,
Ne'er shou'd the Pencil, or the Sister-Muse
Be try'd by those who easily excuse:
But strictest Censors shou'd of either judge,
Applaud the Artist, and despise the Drudge.
Then never wou'd thy Colours have debas'd
CLEONE's Features, and her Charms defac'd:
Nor had my Pen (more subject to their Laws)
Assay'd to vindicate her Beauty's Cause.
A rigid Fear had kept us both in Awe,
Nor I compos'd, nor thou presum'd to draw;
But in CLEONE viewing with Surprize
That Excellence, to which we ne'er cou'd rise,
By less Attempts we safely might have gain'd
That humble Praise which neither has obtain'd,
Since to thy Shadowings, or my ruder Verse,

It is not giv'n to shew, or to rehearse
What Nature in CLEONE's Face has writ,
A soft Endearment, and a chearful Wit,
That all-subduing, that enliv'ning Air
By which, a sympathizing Joy we share,
For who forbears to smile, when smil'd on by the Fair?

A Pastoral DIALOGUE between Two Shepherdesses

Silvia
Pretty Nymph! within this Shade,
Whilst the Flocks to rest are laid,
Whilst the World dissolves in Heat,
Take this cool, and flow'ry Seat:
And with pleasing Talk awhile
Let us two the Time beguile;
Tho' thou here no Shepherd see,
To encline his humble Knee,
Or with melancholy Lays
Sing thy dangerous Beauty's Praise.

Dorinda
Nymph! with thee I here wou'd stay,
But have heard, that on this Day,
Near those Beeches, scarce in view,
All the Swains some Mirth pursue:
To whose meeting now I haste.
Solitude do's Life but waste.

Silvia
Prithee, but a Moment stay.

Dorinda
No! my Chaplet wou'd decay;
Ev'ry drooping Flow'r wou'd mourn,
And wrong the Face, they shou'd adorn.

Silvia
I can tell thee, tho' so Fair,
And dress'd with all that rural Care,
Most of the admiring Swains
Will be absent from the Plains.
Gay Sylvander in the Dance
Meeting with a shrew'd Mischance,
To his Cabin's now confin'd
By Mopsus, who the Strain did bind:

Damon through the Woods do's stray,
Where his Kids have lost their way:
Young Narcissus iv'ry Brow
Rac'd by a malicious Bough,
Keeps the girlish Boy from sight,
Till Time shall do his Beauty right.

Dorinda
Where's Alexis?

Silvia
 —He, alas!
Lies extended on the Grass;
Tears his Garland, raves, despairs,
Mirth and Harmony forswears;
Since he was this Morning shown,
That Delia must not be his Own.

Dorinda
Foolish Swain! such Love to place.

Silvia
On any but Dorinda's Face.

Dorinda
Hasty Nymph! I said not so.

Silvia
No—but I thy Meaning know.
Ev'ry Shepherd thou wou'd'st have
Not thy Lover, but thy Slave;
To encrease thy captive Train,
Never to be lov'd again.

But, since all are now away,
Prithee, but a Moment stay.

Dorinda
No; the Strangers, from the Vale,
Sure will not this Meeting fail;
Graceful one, the other Fair.
He too, with the pensive Air,
Told me, ere he came this way
He was wont to look more Gay.

Silvia
See! how Pride thy Heart inclines
To think, for Thee that Shepherd pines;

When those Words, that reach'd thy Ear,
Chloe was design'd to hear;
Chloe, who did near thee stand,
And his more speaking Looks command.

Dorinda
Now thy Envy makes me smile.
That indeed were worth his while:
Chloe next thyself decay'd,
And no more a courted Maid.

Silvia
Next myself! Young Nymph, forbear.
Still the Swains allow me Fair,
Tho' not what I was that Day,
When Colon bore the Prize away;
When—

Dorinda
—Oh, hold! that Tale will last,
Till all the Evening Sports are past;
Till no Streak of Light is seen,
Nor Footstep prints the flow'ry Green.
What thou wert, I need not know,
What I am, must haste to show.
Only this I now discern
From the things, thou'd'st have me learn,
That Woman-kind's peculiar Joys
From past, or present Beauties rise.

ALCIDOR

While Monarchs in stern Battle strove
  For proud Imperial Sway;
Abandon'd to his milder Love,
Within a silent peaceful Grove,
  Alcidor careless lay.

Some term'd it cold, unmanly Fear;
  Some, Nicety of Sense,
That Drums and Trumpets cou'd not hear,
The sullying Blasts of Powder bear,
  Or with foul Camps dispense.

A patient Martyr to their Scorn,
  And each ill-fashion'd Jest;

The Youth, who but for Love was born,
Remain'd, and thought it vast Return,
  To reign in Cloria's Breast.

But oh! a ruffling Soldier came
  In all the Pomp of War:
The Gazettes long had spoke his Fame;
Now Hautboys his Approach proclaim,
  And draw in Crouds from far.

Cloria unhappily wou'd gaze;
  And as he nearer drew,
The Man of Feather and of Lace
Stopp'd short, and with profound Amaze
  Took all her Charms to view.

A Bow, which from Campaigns he brought,
  And to his Holsters low,
Herself, and the Spectators taught,
That Her the fairest Nymph he thought,
  Of all that form'd the Row.

Next day, ere Phoebus cou'd be seen,
  Or any Gate unbarr'd;
At hers, upon th' adjoining Green,
From Ranks, with waving Flags between,
  Were soften'd Trumpets heard.

The Noon do's following Treats provide,
  In the Pavilion's Shade;
The Neighborhood, and all beside,
That will attend the amorous Pride,
  Are welcom'd with the Maid.

Poor Alcidor! thy Hopes are cross'd,
  Go perish on the Ground;
Thy Sighs by stronger Notes are toss'd,
Drove back, or in the Passage lost;
  Rich Wines thy Tears have drown'd.

In Women's Hearts, the softest Things
  Which Nature cou'd devise,
Are yet some harsh, and jarring Strings,
That, when loud Fame, or Profit rings,
  Will answer to the Noise.

Poor Alcidor! go Fight or Dye;
  Let thy fond Notions cease:

Man was not made in Shades to lie,
Or his full Bliss, at ease, enjoy,
  To Live, or Love in peace.

Some Pieces out of the first ACT of the AMINTA of TASSO

Daphne's Answer to Sylvia, declaring she should esteem all as Enemies, who should talk to her of LOVE

Then, to the snowy Ewe, in thy esteem,
The Father of the Flock a Foe must seem,
The faithful Turtles to their yielding Mates.
The chearful Spring, which Love and Joy creates,
That reconciles the World by soft Desires,
And tender Thoughts in ev'ry Breast inspires,
To you a hateful Season must appear,
Whilst Love prevails, and all are Lovers here.
Observe the gentle Murmurs of that Dove,
And see, how billing she confirms her Love!
For this, the Nightingale displays her Throat,
And Love, Love, Love, is all her Ev'ning Note.
The very Tygers have their tender Hours,
And prouder Lyons bow beneath Love's Pow'rs.
Thou, prouder yet than that imperious Beast,
Alone deny'st him Shelter in thy Breast.
But why should I the Creatures only name
That Sense partake, as Owners of this Flame?
Love farther goes, nor stops his Course at these:
The Plants he moves, and gently bends the Trees.
See how those Willows mix their am'rous Boughs;
And, how that Vine clasps her supporting Spouse!
The silver Firr dotes on the stately Pine;
By Love those Elms, by Love those Beeches join.
But view that Oak; behold his rugged Side:
Yet that rough Bark the melting Flame do's hide.
All, by their trembling Leaves, in Sighs declare
And tell their Passions to the gath'ring Air.
Which, had but Love o'er Thee the least Command,
Thou, by their Motions, too might'st understand.
AMINTOR, being ask'd by THIRSIS Who is the Object of his Love? speaks as follows.

AMINTA
THIRSIS! to Thee I mean that Name to show,
Which, only yet our Groves, and Fountains know:
That, when my Death shall through the Plains be told,
Thou with the wretched Cause may'st that unfold

To every-one, who shall my Story find
Carv'd by thy Hand, in some fair Beeches rind;
Beneath whose Shade the bleeding Body lay:
That, when by chance she shall be led that way,
O'er my sad Grave the haughty Nymph may go,
And the proud Triumph of her Beauty shew
To all the Swains, to Strangers as they pass;
And yet at length she may (but Oh! alas!
I fear, too high my flatt'ring Hopes do soar)
Yet she at length may my sad Fate deplore;
May weep me Dead, may o'er my Tomb recline,
And sighing, wish were he alive and Mine!
But mark me to the End—

THIRSIS
Go on; for well I do thy Speech attend,
Perhaps to better Ends, than yet thou know'st.

AMINTA
Being now a Child, or but a Youth at most,
When scarce to reach the blushing Fruit I knew,
Which on the lowest bending Branches grew;
Still with the dearest, sweetest, kindest Maid
Young as myself, at childish Sports I play'd.
The Fairest, sure, of all that Lovely Kind,
Who spread their golden Tresses to the Wind;
Cydippe's Daughter, and Montano's Heir,
Whose Flocks and Herds so num'rous do appear;
The beauteous Sylvia; She, 'tis She I love,
Warmth of all Hearts, and Pride of ev'ry Grove.
With Her I liv'd, no Turtles e'er so fond.
Our Houses met, but more our Souls were join'd.
Together Nets for Fish, and Fowl we laid;
Together through the spacious Forest stray'd;
Pursu'd with equal Speed the flying Deer,
And of the Spoils there no Divisions were.
But whilst I from the Beasts their Freedom won,
Alas! I know not how, my Own was gone.
By unperceiv'd Degrees the Fire encreas'd,
Which fill'd, at last, each corner of my Breast;
As from a Root, tho' scarce discern'd so small,
A Plant may rise, that grows amazing tall.
From Sylvia's Presence now I could not move,
And from her Eyes took in full Draughts of Love,
Which sweetly thro' my ravish'd Mind distill'd;
Yet in the end such Bitterness wou'd yield,
That oft I sigh'd, ere yet I knew the cause,
And was a Lover, ere I dream'd I was.

But Oh! at last, too well my State I knew;
And now, will shew thee how this Passion grew.
Then listen, while the pleasing Tale I tell.

THIRSIS persuades AMINTOR not to despair upon the Predictions of Mopsus discov'ring him to be an Impostor

THIRSIS
Why dost thou still give way to such Despair!

AMINTOR
Too just, alas! the weighty Causes are.
Mopsus, wise Mopsus, who in Art excels,
And of all Plants the secret Vertue tells,
Knows, with what healing Gifts our Springs abound,
And of each Bird explains the mystick Sound;
'Twas He, ev'n He! my wretched Fate foretold.

THIRSIS
Dost thou this Speech then of that Mopsus hold,
Who, whilst his Smiles attract the easy View,
Drops flatt'ring Words, soft as the falling Dew;
Whose outward Form all friendly still appears,
Tho' Fraud and Daggers in his Thoughts he wears,
And the unwary Labours to surprize
With Looks affected, and with riddling Lyes.
If He it is, that bids thy Love despair,
I hope the happier End of all thy Care.
So far from Truth his vain Predictions fall.

AMINTOR
If ought thou know'st, that may my Hopes recall,
Conceal it not; for great I've heard his Fame,
And fear'd his Words—

THIRSIS
—When hither first I came,
And in these Shades the false Imposter met,
Like Thee I priz'd, and thought his Judgment great;
On all his study'd Speeches still rely'd,
Nor fear'd to err, whilst led by such a Guide:
When on a Day, that Bus'ness and Delight
My Steps did to the Neighb'ring Town invite,
Which stands upon that rising Mountain's side,
And from our Plains this River do's divide,
He check'd me thus—Be warn'd in time, My Son,
And that new World of painted Mischiefs shun,

Whose gay Inhabitants thou shalt behold
Plum'd like our Birds, and sparkling all in Gold;
Courtiers, that will thy rustick Garb despise,
And mock thy Plainness with disdainful Eyes.
But above all, that Structure see thou fly,
Where hoarded Vanities and Witchcrafts lie;
To shun that Path be thy peculiar Care.
I ask, what of that Place the Dangers are:
To which he soon replies, there shalt thou meet
Of soft Enchantresses th' Enchantments sweet,
Who subt'ly will thy solid Sense bereave,
And a false Gloss to ev'ry Object give.
Brass to thy Sight as polish'd Gold shall seem,
And Glass thou as the Diamond shalt esteem.

Huge Heaps of Silver to thee shall appear,
Which if approach'd, will prove but shining Air.
The very Walls by Magick Art are wrought,
And Repitition to all Speakers taught:
Not such, as from our Ecchoes we obtain,
Which only our last Words return again;
But Speech for Speech entirely there they give,
And often add, beyond what they receive.
There downy Couches to false Rest invite,
The Lawn is charm'd, that faintly bars the Light.
No gilded Seat, no iv'ry Board is there,
But what thou may'st for some Delusion fear:
Whilst, farther to abuse thy wond'ring Eyes,
Strange antick Shapes before them shall arise;
Fantastick Fiends, that will about thee flock,
And all they see, with Imitation mock.
Nor are these Ills the worst. Thyself may'st be
Transform'd into a Flame, a Stream, a Tree;
A Tear, congeal'd by Art, thou may'st remain,
'Till by a burning Sigh dissolv'd again.

Thus spake the Wretch; but cou'd not shake my Mind.
My way I take, and soon the City find,
Where above all that lofty Fabrick stands,
Which, with one View, the Town and Plains commands.
Here was I stopt, for who cou'd quit the Ground,
That heard such Musick from those Roofs resound!
Musick! beyond th' enticing Syrene's Note;
Musick! beyond the Swan's expiring Throat;
Beyond the softest Voice, that charms the Grove,
And equal'd only by the Spheres above.
My Ear I thought too narrow for the Art,
Nor fast enough convey'd it to my Heart:

When in the Entrance of the Gate I saw
A Man Majestick, and commanding Awe;
Yet temper'd with a Carriage, so refin'd
That undetermin'd was my doubtful Mind,
Whether for Love, or War, that Form was most design'd.

With such a Brow, as did at once declare
A gentle Nature, and a Wit severe;
To view that Palace me he ask'd to go,
Tho' Royal He, and I Obscure and Low.
But the Delights my Senses there did meet,
No rural Tongue, no Swain can e'er repeat.
Celestial Goddesses, or Nymphs as Fair,
In unveil'd Beauties, to all Eyes appear
Sprinkl'd with Gold, as glorious to the View,
As young Aurora, deck'd with pearly Dew;
Bright Rays dispensing, as along they pass'd,
And with new Light the shining Palace grac'd.
Phoebus was there by all the Muses met,
And at his Feet was our Elpino set.
Ev'n humble Me their Harmony inspir'd,
My Breast expanded, and my Spirits fir'd.
Rude Past'ral now, no longer I rehearse,
But Heroes crown with my exalted Verse.
Of Arms I sung, of bold advent'rous Wars;
And tho' brought back by my too envious Stars,
Yet kept my Voice and Reed those lofty Strains,
And sent loud Musick through the wond'ring Plains:
Which Mopsus hearing, secretly malign'd,
And now to ruin Both at once design'd.
Which by his Sorceries he soon brought to pass;
And suddenly so clogg'd, and hoarse I was,
That all our Shepherds, at the Change amaz'd,
Believ'd, I on some Ev'ning-Wolf had gaz'd:
When He it was, my luckless Path had crost,
By whose dire Look, my Skill awhile was lost.
This have I told, to raise thy Hopes again,
And render, by distrust, his Malice vain.

From the AMINTA of TASSO

Tho' we, of small Proportion see
And slight the armed Golden Bee;
Yet if her Sting behind she leaves,
No Ease th' envenom'd Flesh receives.

Love, less to Sight than is this Fly,
In a soft Curl conceal'd can lie;
Under an Eyelid's lovely Shade,
Can form a dreadful Ambuscade;
Can the most subtil Sight beguile
Hid in the Dimples of a Smile.
But if from thence a Dart he throw,
How sure, how mortal is the Blow!
How helpless all the Pow'r of Art
To bind, or to restore the Heart!

From the AMINTA of TASSO

Part of the Description of the Golden Age

Then, by some Fountains flow'ry side
The Loves unarm'd, did still abide.
Then, the loos'd Quiver careless hung,
The Torch extinct, the Bow unstrung.

Then, by the Nymphs no Charms were worn,
But such as with the Nymphs were born.
The Shepherd cou'd not, then, complain,
Nor told his am'rous Tale in vain.
No Veil the Beauteous Face did hide,
Nor harmless Freedom was deny'd.
Then, Innocence and Virtue reign'd
Pure, unaffected, unconstrain'd.
Love was their Pleasure, and their Praise,
The soft Employment of their Days.

To The NIGHTINGALE

Exert thy Voice, sweet Harbinger of Spring!
   This Moment is thy Time to sing,
   This Moment I attend to Praise,
And set my Numbers to thy Layes.
   Free as thine shall be my Song;
   As thy Musick, short, or long.

Poets, wild as thee, were born,
   Pleasing best when unconfin'd,
   When to Please is least design'd,
Soothing but their Cares to rest;

Cares do still their Thoughts molest,
And still th' unhappy Poet's Breast,
Like thine, when best he sings, is plac'd against a Thorn.
She begins, Let all be still!
Muse, thy Promise now fulfill!
Sweet, oh! sweet, still sweeter yet
Can thy Words such Accents fit,
Canst thou Syllables refine,
Melt a Sense that shall retain
Still some Spirit of the Brain,
Till with Sounds like these it join.
'Twill not be! then change thy Note;
Let division shake thy Throat.
Hark! Division now she tries;
Yet as far the Muse outflies.

Cease then, prithee, cease thy Tune;
Trifler, wilt thou sing till June?
Till thy Bus'ness all lies waste,
And the Time of Building's past!
Thus we Poets that have Speech,
Unlike what thy Forests teach,
If a fluent Vein be shown
That's transcendant to our own,
Criticize, reform, or preach,
Or censure what we cannot reach.

The ATHEIST and the ACORN

Methinks this World is oddly made,
And ev'ry thing's amiss,
A dull presuming Atheist said,
As stretch'd he lay beneath a Shade;
And instanced in this:

Behold, quoth he, that mighty thing,
A Pumpkin, large and round,
Is held but by a little String,
Which upwards cannot make it spring,
Or bear it from the Ground.

Whilst on this Oak, a Fruit so small,
So disproportion'd, grows;
That, who with Sence surveys this All,
This universal Casual Ball,
Its ill Contrivance knows.

My better Judgment wou'd have hung
  That Weight upon a Tree,
And left this Mast, thus slightly strung,
'Mongst things which on the Surface sprung,
  And small and feeble be.

No more the Caviller cou'd say,
  Nor farther Faults descry;
For, as he upwards gazing lay,
An Acorn, loosen'd from the Stay,
  Fell down upon his Eye.

Th' offended Part with Tears ran o'er,
  As punish'd for the Sin:
Fool! had that Bough a Pumpkin bore,
Thy Whimseys must have work'd no more,
  Nor Scull had kept them in.

The Tradesman and the Scholar

A Citizen of mighty Pelf,
But much a Blockhead, in himself
Disdain'd a Man of shining Parts,
Master of Sciences and Arts,
Who left his Book scarce once a day
For sober Coffee, Smoak, or Tea;
Nor spent more Money in the Town
Than bought, when need requir'd, a Gown;
Which way of Living much offends
The Alderman, who gets and spends,
And grudges him the Vital Air,
Who drives no Trade, and takes no Care.
Why Bookworm! to him once he cry'd,
Why, setting thus the World aside,
Dost thou thy useless Time consume,
Enclos'd within a lonely Room,
And poring damnify thy Wit,
'Till not for Men, or Manners fit?
Hop'st thou, with urging of thy Vein,
To spin a Fortune from thy Brain?
Or gain a Patron, that shall raise
Thy solid State, for empty Praise?
No; trust not to your Soothings vile,
Receiv'd per me's the only Stile.
Your Book's but frown'd on by My Lord;

If Mine's uncross'd, I reach his Board.

In slighting Yours, he shuts his Hand;
Protracting Mine, devolves the Land.
Then let Advantage be the Test,
Which of us Two ev'n Writes the best.
Besides, I often Scarlet wear,
And strut to Church, just next the Mayor.
Whilst rusty Black, with Inch of Band,
Is all the Dress you understand;
Who in the Pulpit thresh to Please,
Whilst I below can snore at Ease.
Yet, if you prove me there a Sinner,
I let you go without a Dinner.
This Prate was so beneath the Sence
Of One, who Wisdom cou'd dispense,
Unheard, or unreturn'd it past:
But War now lays the City waste,
And plunder'd Goods profusely fell
By length of Pike, not length of Ell.
Abroad th' Inhabitants are forc'd,
From Shops, and Trade, and Wealth divorc'd.

The Student leaving but his Book,
The Tumult of the Place forsook.
In Foreign Parts, One tells his Tale,
How Rich he'd been, how quick his Sale,
Which do's for scanty Alms prevail.
The Chance of War whilst he deplores,
And dines at Charitable Doors;
The Man of Letters, known by Fame,
Was welcom'd, wheresoe'er he came.
Still, Potentates entreat his Stay,
Whose Coaches meet him on the Way:
And Universities contest
Which shall exceed, or use him best.
Amaz'd the Burgomaster sees
On Foot, and scorn'd such Turns as these;
And sighing, now deplores too late
His cumb'rous Trash, and shallow Pate:
Since loaded but with double Chest
Of learned Head, and honest Breast,
The Scholar moves from Place to Place,
And finds in every Climate Grace.
Wit and the Arts, on that Foundation rais'd,
(Howe'er the Vulgar are with Shows amaz'd)
Is all that recommends, or can be justly prais'd.

Man's Injustice Towards Providence

A Thriving Merchant, who no Loss sustained,
In little time a mighty Fortune gain'd.
No Pyrate seiz'd his still returning Freight;
Nor foundring Vessel sunk with its own Weight:
No Ruin enter'd through dissever'd Planks;
No Wreck at Sea, nor in the Publick Banks.
Aloft he sails, above the Reach of Chance,
And do's in Pride, as fast as Wealth, advance.
His Wife too, had her Town and Country-Seat,
And rich in Purse, concludes her Person Great.
A Dutchess wears not so much Gold and Lace;
Then 'tis with Her an undisputed Case,
The finest Petticoat must take the Place.
Her Rooms, anew at ev'ry Christ'ning drest,
Put down the Court, and vex the City-Guest.
Grinning Malottos in true Ermin stare;
The best Japan, and clearest China Ware
Are but as common Delft and English Laquar there.
No Luxury's by either unenjoy'd,
Or cost withheld, tho' awkardly employ'd.
How comes this Wealth? A Country Friend demands,
Who scarce cou'd live on Product of his Lands.
How is it that, when Trading is so bad
That some are Broke, and some with Fears run Mad,
You can in better State yourself maintain,
And your Effects still unimpair'd remain!
My Industry, he cries, is all the Cause;
Sometimes I interlope, and slight the Laws;
I wiser Measures, than my Neighbors, take,
And better speed, who better Bargains make.
I knew, the Smyrna–Fleet wou'd fall a Prey,
And therefore sent no Vessel out that way:
My busy Factors prudently I chuse,
And in streight Bonds their Friends and Kindred noose:
At Home, I to the Publick Sums advance,
Whilst, under-hand in Fee with hostile France,
I care not for your Tourvills, or Du-Barts,
No more than for the Rocks, and Shelves in Charts:
My own sufficiency creates my Gain,
Rais'd, and secur'd by this unfailing Brain.
This idle Vaunt had scarcely past his Lips,
When Tydings came, his ill-provided Ships
Some thro' the want of Skill, and some of Care,
Were lost, or back return'd without their Fare.

From bad to worse, each Day his State declin'd,
'Till leaving Town, and Wife, and Debts behind,
To his Acquaintance at the Rural Seat
He Sculks, and humbly sues for a Retreat.
Whence comes this Change, has Wisdom left that Head,
(His Friend demands) where such right Schemes were bred?
What Phrenzy, what Delirium mars the Scull,
Which fill'd the Chests, and was it self so full?
Here interrupting, sadly he Reply'd,
In Me's no Change, but Fate must all Things guide;
To Providence I attribute my Loss.
Vain-glorious Man do's thus the Praise engross,
When Prosp'rous Days around him spread their Beams:
But, if revolv'd to opposite Extreams,
Still his own Sence he fondly will prefer,
And Providence, not He, in his Affairs must Err!

The Eagle, the Sow, and the Cat

The Queen of Birds, t'encrease the Regal Stock,
Had hatch'd her young Ones in a stately Oak,
Whose Middle-part was by a Cat possest,
And near the Root with Litter warmly drest,
A teeming Sow had made her peaceful Nest.
(Thus Palaces are cramm'd from Roof to Ground,
And Animals, as various, in them found.)
When to the Sow, who no Misfortune fear'd,
Puss with her fawning Compliments appear'd,
Rejoicing much at her Deliv'ry past,
And that she 'scap'd so well, who bred so fast.
Then every little Piglin she commends,
And likens them to all their swinish Friends;
Bestows good Wishes, but with Sighs implies,
That some dark Fears do in her Bosom rise.
Such Tempting Flesh, she cries, will Eagles spare?
Methinks, good Neighbour, you should live in Care:
Since I, who bring not forth such dainty Bits,
Tremble for my unpalatable Chits;
And had I but foreseen, the Eagle's Bed
Was in this fatal Tree to have been spread;
I sooner wou'd have kitten'd in the Road,
Than made this Place of Danger my abode.
I heard her young Ones lately cry for Pig,
And pity'd you, that were so near, and big.
In Friendship this I secretly reveal,
Lest Pettitoes shou'd make th' ensuing Meal;

Or else, perhaps, Yourself may be their aim,
For a Sow's Paps has been a Dish of Fame.
No more the sad, affrighted Mother hears,
But overturning all with boist'rous Fears,
She from her helpless Young in haste departs,
Whilst Puss ascends, to practice farther Arts.
The Anti-chamber pass'd, she scratch'd the Door;
The Eagle, ne'er alarum'd so before,
Bids her come in, and look the Cause be great,
That makes her thus disturb the Royal Seat;
Nor think, of Mice and Rats some pest'ring Tale
Shall, in excuse of Insolence, prevail.
Alas! my Gracious Lady, quoth the Cat,
I think not of such Vermin; Mouse, or Rat
To me are tasteless grown; nor dare I stir
To use my Phangs, or to expose my Fur.
A Foe intestine threatens all around,
And ev'n this lofty Structure will confound;
A Pestilential Sow, a meazel'd Pork
On the Foundation has been long at work,
Help'd by a Rabble, issu'd from her Womb,
Which she has foster'd in that lower Room;
Who now for Acorns are so madly bent,
That soon this Tree must fall, for their Content.
I wou'd have fetch'd some for th' unruly Elves;
But 'tis the Mob's delight to help Themselves:
Whilst your high Brood must with the meanest drop,
And steeper be their Fall, as next the Top;
Unless you soon to Jupiter repair,
And let him know, the Case demands his Care.
Oh! May the Trunk but stand, 'till you come back!
But hark! already sure, I hear it crack.
Away, away---The Eagle, all agast,
Soars to the Sky, nor falters in her haste:
Whilst crafty Puss, now o'er the Eyry reigns,
Replenishing her Maw with treach'rous Gains.
The Sow she plunders next, and lives alone;
The Pigs, the Eaglets, and the House her own.

Curs'd Sycophants! How wretched is the Fate
Of those, who know you not, till 'tis too late!

To a Friend, in Praise of the Invention of Writing Letters

Blest be the Man! his Memory at least,
Who found the Art, thus to unfold his Breast,

And taught succeeding Times an easy way
Their secret Thoughts by Letters to convey;
To baffle Absence, and secure Delight,
Which, till that Time, was limited to Sight.
The parting Farewel spoke, the last Adieu,
The less'ning Distance past, then loss of View,
The Friend was gone, which some kind Moments gave,
And Absence separated, like the Grave
The Wings of Love were tender too, till then
No Quill, thence pull'd, was shap'd into a Pen,
To send in Paper-sheets, from Town to Town,
Words smooth was they, and softer than his Down.
O'er such he reign'd, whom Neighborhood had join'd,
And hopt, from Bough to Bough, supported by the Wind.
When for a Wife the youthful Patriarch sent,
The Camels, Jewels, and the Steward went,
A wealthy Equipage, tho' grave and slow;
But not a Line, that might the Lover shew.
The Rings and Bracelets woo'd her Hands and Arms;
But had she known of melting Words, the Charms
That under secret Seals in Ambush lie,
To catch the Soul, when drawn into the Eye,
The Fair Assyrian had not took this Guide,
Nor her soft Heart in Chains of Pearl been ty'd.
  Had these Conveyances been then in Date,
Joseph had known his wretched Father's State,
Before a Famine, which his Life pursues,
Had sent his other Sons, to tell the News.
  Oh! might I live to see an Art arise,
As this to Thoughts, indulgent to the Eyes;
That the dark Pow'rs of distance cou'd subdue,
And make me See, as well as Talk to You;
That tedious Miles, nor Tracts of Air might prove
Bars to my Sight, and shadows to my Love!
Yet were it granted, such unbounded Things
Are wand'ring Wishes, born on Phancy's Wings,
They'd stretch themselves beyond this happy Case,
And ask an Art, to help us to Embrace.

A Miller, His Son, and their Ass

A FABLE Translated from Monsieur de la Fontaine

Tho' to Antiquity the Praise we yield
Of pleasing Arts; and Fable's earli'st Field
Own to be fruitful Greece; yet not so clean

Those Ears were reap'd, but still there's some to glean;
And from the Lands of vast Invention come
Daily new Authors, with Discov'ries home.
  This curious Piece, which I shall now impart,
Fell from Malherbe, a Master in his Art,
To Racan, fill'd with like poetick Fire,
Both tuneful Servants of Apollo's Choir:
Rivals and Heirs to the Horatian Lyre:
Who meeting him, one Day, free and alone,
(For still their Thoughts were to each other known)
Thus ask'd his Aid—Some useful Counsel give,
Thou who, by living long, hast learnt to live;
Whose Observation nothing can escape;
Tell me, how I my course of Life shall shape:
To something I wou'd fix ere't be too late.
You know my Birth, my Talents, my Estate:
Shall I with these content, all Search resign,
And to the Country my Desires confine?
Or in the Court, or Camp, advancement gain?
The World's a mixture of Delight and Pain:
Tho' rough it seems, there's Pleasure in the Wars,
And Hymen's Joys are not without their Cares.
I need not ask, to what my Genius tends,
But wou'd content the World, the Court, my Friends.
  Please all the World (in haste) Malherbe replies?
How vain th' Attempt will prove in him, that tries,
Learn from a Fable, I have somewhere found,
Before I answer all that you propound.

  A Miller and his Son (the Father old,
The Boy about some fifteen Years had told)
Designed their Ass to sell, and for the Fair,
Some distance off, accordingly prepare.
But lest she in the walk should lose her Flesh,
And not appear, for Sale, so full and fresh,
Her Feet together ty'd; between them two
They heav'd her up; and on the Rusticks go:
Till those, who met them bearing thus the Ass,
Cry'd, Are these Fools about to act a Farce?
Surely the Beast (howe'er it seem to be)
Is not the greatest Ass of all the Three.
The Miller in their Mirth his Folly finds,
And down he sets her, and again unbinds;
And tho' her grumbling shew'd, she lik'd much more
The lazy way, she travell'd in before,
He minds her not; but up the Boy he sets
Upon her Back, and on the Crupper gets.
Thus on they jog, when of Three Men that pass'd,

The eldest thinking Age to be disgrac'd,
Call'd to the Youth, ho! you, young Man for shame!
Come down, lest Passengers your Manners blame,
And say, it ill becomes your tender Years
To ride before a Grandsire with grey Hairs.
Truly, the Gentlemen are in the right,
The Miller cries, and makes the Boy alight;
Then forward slides himself into his place,
And with a Mind content renews his pace:
But much he had not gain'd upon his way,
Before a Troop of Damsels, neat and gay,
(Partial to Youth) to one another cry'd,
See, how with walking by that Dotard's side,
The Boy is tir'd; whilst with a Prelate's state
He rides alone, and dangling in the Seat,
Hangs like a Calf thrown up, across the Beast.
The Miller, thinking to have spoiled that Jest,
Reply'd, he was too Old for Veal to pass,
But after more on him, and on his Ass,
He stands convinc'd, and takes his Son again
To ride at ease himself, still next the Mane.
Yet ere he'd thirty Paces borne the Lad,
The next they met, cry'd---Are these Fellows mad!
Have they no Pity thus t'o'erload the Jade!
Sure, at the Fair, they for her Skin may trade.
See, how's she spent, and sinks beneath their strokes!
The Miller, whom this most of all provokes,
Swears by his Cap, he shews his want of Brains,
Who thus to please the World, bestows his Pains.
Howe'er we'll try, if this way't may be done;
And off he comes, and fetches down his Son.
Behind they walk, and now the Creature drive,
But cou'd no better in their Purpose thrive;
Nor scape a Fellow's Censure, whom they meet,
That cries, to spare the Ass they break their Feet;
And whilst unladen at her ease she goes,
Trudge in the Dirt, and batter out their Shooes;
As if to burthen her they were afraid,
And Men for Beasts, not Beasts for Men were made.

The Proverb right, the Cart before the Horse.
The Miller, finding things grow worse and worse,
Cries out, I am an Ass, it is agreed,
And so are all, who wou'd in this succeed.
Hereafter, tho' Reproof or Praise I find,
I'll neither heed, but follow my own Mind,
Take my own Counsel, how my Beast to sell.
This he resolv'd, and did it, and did well.

For you, Sir, Follow Love, the Court, the War;
Obtain the Crosier, or the City's Furr;
Live single all your Days, or take a Wife;
Trust me, a Censure waits each state of Life.

The Man Bitten by Fleas

A Peevish Fellow laid his Head
  On Pillows, stuff'd with Down;
But was no sooner warm in Bed,
  With hopes to rest his Crown,

But Animals of slender size,
  That feast on humane Gore,
From secret Ambushes arise,
  Nor suffer him to snore;

Who starts, and scrubs, and frets, and swears,
  'Till, finding all in vain,
He for Relief employs his Pray'rs
  In this old Heathen strain.

Great Jupiter! thy Thunder send
  From out the pitchy Clouds,
And give these Foes a dreadful End,
  That lurk in Midnight Shrouds:

Or Hercules might with a Blow,
  If once together brought,
This Crew of Monsters overthrow,
  By which such Harms are wrought.

The Strife, ye Gods! is worthy You,
  Since it our Blood has cost;
And scorching Fevers must ensue,
  When cooling Sleep is lost.

Strange Revolutions wou'd abound,
  Did Men ne'er close their Eyes;
Whilst those, who wrought them wou'd be found
  At length more Mad, than Wise.

Passive Obedience must be us'd,
  If this cannot be Cur'd;
But whilst one Flea is slowly bruis'd,
  Thousands must be endur'd.

Confusion, Slav'ry, Death and Wreck
  Will on the Nation seize,
If, whilst you keep your Thunders back,
  We're massacr'd by Fleas.

Why, prithee, shatter-headed Fop,
  The laughing Gods reply;
Hast thou forgot thy Broom, and Mop,
  And Wormwood growing nigh?

Go sweep, and wash, and strew thy Floor,
  As all good Housewives teach;
And do not thus for Thunders roar,
  To make some fatal Breach:

Which You, nor your succeeding Heir,
  Nor yet a long Descent
Shall find out Methods to repair,
  Tho' Prudence may prevent.

For Club, and Bolts, a Nation call'd of late,
Nor wou'd be eas'd by Engines of less Weight:
But whether lighter had not done as well,
Let their Great-Grandsons, or their Grandsons tell.

REFORMATION

A Gentleman, most wretched in his Lot,
A wrangling and reproving Wife had got,
Who, tho' she curb'd his Pleasures, and his Food,
Call'd him My Dear, and did it for his Good,
Ills to prevent; She of all Ills the worst,
So wisely Froward, and so kindly Curst.
The Servants too experiment her Lungs,
And find they've Breath to serve a thousand Tongues.
Nothing went on; for her eternal Clack
Still rectifying, set all Matters back;
Nor Town, nor Neighbours, nor the Court cou'd please,
But furnish'd Matter for her sharp Disease.
To distant Plains at length he gets her down,
With no Affairs to manage of her own;
Hoping from that unactive State to find
A calmer Habit, grown upon her Mind:
But soon return'd he hears her at his Door,
As noisy and tempestuous as before;

Yet mildly ask'd, How she her Days had spent
Amidst the Quiet of a sweet Content,
Where Shepherds 'tend their Flocks, and Maids their Pails,
And no harsh Mistress domineers, or rails?
Not rail! she cries—Why, I that had no share
In their Concerns, cou'd not the Trollops spare;
But told 'em, they were Sluts—And for the Swains,
My Name a Terror to them still remains;
So often I reprov'd their slothful Faults,
And with such Freedom told 'em all my Thoughts,
That I no more amongst them cou'd reside.
Has then, alas! the Gentleman reply'd,
One single Month so much their patience try'd?
Where you by Day, and but at Seasons due,
Cou'd with your Clamours their Defects pursue;
How had they shrunk, and justly been afraid,
Had they with me one Curtain Lecture heard!
Yet enter Madam, and resume your Sway;
Who can't Command, must silently Obey.
In secret here let endless Faults be found,
Till, like Reformers who in States abound,
You all to Ruin bring, and ev'ry Part confound.

Fragment at Tunbridge-Wells

For He, that made, must new create us,
Ere Seneca, or Epictetus,
With all their serious Admonitions,
Can, for the Spleen, prove good Physicians.
The Heart's unruly Palpitation
Will not be laid by a Quotation;
Nor will the Spirits move the lighter
For the most celebrated Writer.
Sweats, Swoonings, and convulsive Motions
Will not be cur'd by Words, and Notions.

Then live, old Brown! with thy Chalybeats,
Which keep us from becoming Idiots.
At Tunbridge let us still be Drinking,
Though 'tis the Antipodes to Thinking:
Such Hurry, whilst the Spirit's flying,
Such Stupefaction, when 'tis dying;
Yet these, and not sententious Papers,
Must brighten Life, and cure the Vapours, &c.

A Pindarick Poem

Upon the Hurricane in November 1703, referring to this Text in Psalm 148. ver. 8. Winds and Storms fulfilling his Word

With a HYMN compos'd of the 148th PSALM Paraphras'd

You have obey'd, you WINDS, that must fulfill
  The Great Disposer's righteous Will;
Throughout the Land, unlimited you flew,
Nor sought, as heretofore, with Friendly Aid
  Only, new Motion to bestow
Upon the sluggish Vapours, bred below,
Condensing into Mists, and melancholy Shade.
  No more such gentle Methods you pursue,
  But marching now in terrible Array,
   Undistinguish'd was your Prey:
  In vain the Shrubs, with lowly Bent,
  Sought their Destruction to prevent;
  The Beech in vain, with out-stretch'd Arms,
  Deprecates th' approaching Harms;
  In vain the Oak (so often storm'd)
  Rely'd upon that native Force,
  By which already was perform'd
  So much of his appointed Course,
  As made him, fearless of Decay,
   Wait but the accomplish'd Time
  Of his long-wish'd and useful Prime,
To be remov'd, with Honor, to the Sea.

  The strait and ornamental Pine
  Did in the like Ambition joyn,
  And thought his Fame shou'd ever last,
When in some Royal Ship he stood the planted Mast;
  And shou'd again his Length of Timber rear,
  And new engrafted Branches wear
  Of fibrous Cordage and impending Shrouds,
Still trimm'd with human Care, and water'd by the Clouds.
  But oh, you Trees! who solitary stood;
   Or you, whose Numbers form'd a Wood;
   You, who on Mountains chose to rise,
   And drew them nearer to the Skies;
   Or you, whom Valleys late did hold
   In flexible and lighter Mould;
You num'rous Brethren of the Leafy Kind,
  To whatsoever Use design'd,
  Now, vain you found it to contend

With not, alas! one Element; your Friend
Your Mother Earth, thro' long preceding Rains,
  (Which undermining sink below)
 No more her wonted Strength retains;
Nor you so fix'd within her Bosom grow,
 That for your sakes she can resolve to bear
   These furious Shocks of hurrying Air;
But finding All your Ruin did conspire,
She soon her beauteous Progeny resign'd
To this destructive, this imperious Wind,
That check'd your nobler Aims, and gives you to the Fire.
 Thus! have thy Cedars, Libanus, been struck
   As the lythe Oziers twisted round;
 Thus! Cadez, has thy Wilderness been shook,
 When the appalling, and tremendous Sound
   Of rattl'ing Tempests o'er you broke,
   And made your stubborn Glories bow,
 When in such Whirlwinds the Almighty spoke,
Warning Judea then, as our Britannia now.

 Yet these were the remoter Harms,
 Foreign the Care, and distant the Alarms:
   Whilst but sheltring Trees alone,
   Master'd soon, and soon o'erthrown,
   Felt those Gusts, which since prevail,
   And loftier Palaces assail;
   Whose shaken Turrets now give way,
 With vain Inscriptions, which the Freeze has borne
 Through Ages past, t'extol and to adorn,
   And to our latter Times convey;
 Who did the Structures deep Foundation lay,
 Forcing his Praise upon the gazing Croud,
 And, whilst he moulders in a scanty Shroud,
Telling both Earth and Skies, he when alive was proud.
 Now down at once comes the superfluous Load,
   The costly Fret-work with it yields,
 Whose imitated Fruits and Flow'rs are strew'd,
Like those of real Growth o'er the Autumnal Fields.

 The present Owner lifts his Eyes,
 And the swift Change with sad Affrightment spies:
   The Cieling gone, that late the Roof conceal'd;
   The Roof untyl'd, thro' which the Heav'ns reveal'd,
Exposes now his Head, when all Defence has fail'd.

 What alas, is to be done!
 Those, who in Cities wou'd from Dangers run,
   Do but encreasing Dangers meet,

And Death, in various shapes, attending in the Street;
　　While some, too tardy in their Flight,
　　O'ertaken by a worse Mischance,
　　Their upward Parts do scarce advance,
When on their following Limbs th' extending Ruins light.
　One half's interr'd, the other yet survives,
　And for Release with fainting Vigour strives;
　Implores the Aid of absent Friends In vain,
　With fault'ring Speech, and dying Wishes calls
　Those, whom perhaps, their own Domestick Walls
By parallel Distress, or swifter Death retains.
　O Wells! thy Bishop's Mansion we lament,
　So tragical the Fall, so dire th'Event!
　　But let no daring Thought presume
　To point a Cause for that oppressive Doom.
　Yet strictly pious KEN! had'st Thou been there,
　This Fate, we think, had not become thy share;
　　Nor had that awful Fabrick bow'd,
　　Sliding from its loosen'd Bands;
　　Nor yielding Timbers been allow'd
　　To crush thy ever-lifted Hands,
　　　Or interrupt thy Pray'r.
　Those Orizons, that nightly Watches keep,
Had call'd thee from thy Bed, or there secur'd thy Sleep.

　Whilst you, bold Winds and Storms! his Word obey'd,
　Whilst you his Scourge the Great Jehova made,
And into ruin'd Heaps our Edifices laid.
　You South and West the Tragedy began,
As, with disorder'd haste, you o'er the Surface ran;
　　Forgetting, that you were design'd
　(Chiefly thou Zephyrus, thou softest Wind!)
　Only our Heats, when sultry, to allay,
And chase the od'rous Gums by your dispersing Play.
　　Now, by new Orders and Decrees,
　　For our Chastisement issu'd forth,
　You on his Confines the alarmed North
　　With equal Fury sees,
　　And summons swiftly to his Aid
　　Eurus, his Confederate made,
　His eager Second in th' opposing Fight,
　That even the Winds may keep the Balance right,
Nor yield increase of Sway to arbitrary Might.

　Meeting now, they all contend,
　Those assail, while These defend;
　Fierce and turbulent the War,
　And in the loud tumultuous Jar

Winds their own Fifes, and Clarions are.
Each Cavity, which Art or Nature leaves,
Their Inspiration hastily receives;
    Whence, from their various Forms and Size,
    As various Symphonies arise,
Their Trumpet ev'ry hollow Tube is made,
And, when more solid Bodies they invade,
    Enrag'd, they can no farther come,
The beaten Flatt, whilst it repels the Noise,
Resembles but with more outrageous Voice
        The Soldier's threatning Drum:
And when they compass thus our World around,
    When they our Rocks and Mountains rend,
When they our Sacred Piles to their Foundations send,
  No wonder if our ecchoing Caves rebound;
  No wonder if our list'ning Sense they wound,
When arm'd with so much Force, and usher'd with such Sound.
  Nor scarce, amidst the Terrors of that Night,
    When you, fierce Winds, such Desolations wrought,
When you from out his Stores the Great Commander brought,
    Cou'd the most Righteous stand upright;
    Scarcely the Holiest Man performs
    The Service, that becomes it best,
  By ardent Vows, or solemn Pray'rs addrest;
  Nor finds the Calm, so usual to his Breast,
        Full Proof against such Storms.
    How shou'd the Guilty then be found,
  The Men in Wine, or looser Pleasures drown'd,
To fix a stedfast Hope, or to maintain their Ground!
  When at his Glass the late Companion feels,
That Giddy, like himself, the tott'ring Mansion reels!

    The Miser, who with many a Chest
    His gloomy Tenement opprest,
    Now fears the over-burthen'd Floor,
And trembles for his Life, but for his Treasure more.
  What shall he do, or to what Pow'rs apply?
    To those, which threaten from on High,
    By him ne'er call'd upon before,
Who also will suggest th' impossible Restore?
  No; Mammon, to thy Laws he will be true,
And, rather than his Wealth, will bid the World adieu.
  The Rafters sink, and bury'd with his Coin
  That Fate does with his living Thoughts combine;
For still his Heart's inclos'd within a Golden Mine.
    Contention with its angry Brawls
    By Storms o'er-clamour'd, shrinks and falls;
Nor WHIG, nor TORY now the rash Contender calls.

Those, who but Vanity allow'd,
  Nor thought, it reach'd the Name of Sin,
  To be of their Perfections proud,
Too much adorn'd without, or too much rais'd within,
  Now find, that even the lightest Things,
  As the minuter parts of Air,
  When Number to their Weight addition brings,
  Can, like the small, but numerous Insects Stings,
Can, like th' assembl'd Winds, urge Ruin and Despair.
  Thus You've obey'd, you Winds, that must fulfill
  The Great disposer's Righteous Will:
  Thus did your Breath a strict Enquiry make,
  Thus did you our most secret Sins awake,
  And thus chastis'd their Ill.
  Whilst vainly Those, of a rapacious Mind,
  Fields to other Fields had laid,
  By Force, or by injurious Bargains join'd,
With Fences for their Guard impenetrable made;
  The juster Tempest mocks the wrong,
  And sweeps, in its directed Flight,
  Th' Inclosures of another's Right,
Driving at once the Bounds, and licens'd Herds along.
  The Earth agen one general Scene appears;
  No regular distinction now,
  Betwixt the Grounds for Pasture, or the Plough,
  The Face of Nature wears.
  Free as the Men, who wild Confusion love,
  And lawless Liberty approve,
  Their Fellow-Brutes pursue their way,
  To their own Loss, and disadvantage stray,
As wretched in their Choice, as unadvis'd as They.
  The tim'rous Deer, whilst he forsakes the Park,
  And wanders on, in the misguiding Dark,
  Believes, a Foe from ev'ry unknown Bush
  Will on his trembling Body rush,
  Taking the Winds, that vary in their Notes,
For hot pursuing Hounds with deeply bellowing Throats.

  Th' awaken'd Birds, shook from their nightly Seats,
  Their unavailing Pinions ply,
  Repuls'd, as they attempt to fly
In hopes they might attain to more secure Retreats.
  But, Where ye wilder'd Fowls wou'd You repair?
  When this your happy Portion given,
  Your upward Lot, your Firmament of Heaven,
  Your unentail'd, your undivided Air,
  Where no Proprietor was ever known,

Where no litigious Suits have ever grown,
Whilst none from Star to Star cou'd call the space his Own;
When this no more your middle Flights can bear,
But some rough Blast too far above conveighs,
Or to unquitted Earth confines your weak Essays.
Nor You, nor wiser Man cou'd find Repose,
Nor cou'd our Industry produce
Expedients of the smallest Use,
To ward our greater Cares, or mitigate your Woes.

Ye Clouds! that pity'd our Distress,
And by your pacifying Showers
(The soft and usual methods of Success)
Kindly assay'd to make this Tempest less;
Vainly your Aid was now alas! employ'd,
In vain you wept o'er those destructive Hours,
In which the Winds full Tyranny enjoy'd,
Nor wou'd allow you to prevail,
But drove your scorn'd, and scatter'd Tears to wail
The Land that lay destroy'd.
Whilst You obey'd, you Winds! that must fulfill
The just Disposer's Righteous Will;
Whilst not the Earth alone, you disarray,
But to more ruin'd Seas wing'd your impetuous Way.
Which to foreshew, the still portentious Sun
Beamless, and pale of late, his Race begun,
Quenching the Rays, he had no Joy to keep,
In the obscure, and sadly threaten'd Deep.

Farther than we, that Eye of Heaven discerns,
And nearer plac'd to our malignant Stars,
Our brooding Tempests, and approaching Wars
Anticipating learns.
When now, too soon the dark Event
Shews what that faded Planet meant;
Whilst more the liquid Empire undergoes,
More she resigns of her entrusted Stores,
The Wealth, the Strength, the Pride of diff'rent Shores
In one Devoted, one Recorded Night,
Than Years had known destroy'd by generous Fight,
Or Privateering Foes.
All Rules of Conduct laid aside,
No more the baffl'd Pilot steers,
Or knows an Art, when it each moment veers,
To vary with the Winds, or stem th'unusual Tide.
Dispers'd and loose, the shatter'd Vessels stray,
Some perish within sight of Shore,
Some, happier thought, obtain a wider Sea,

But never to return, or cast an Anchor more!
   Some on the Northern Coasts are thrown,
And by congealing Surges compass'd round,
   To fixt and certain Ruin bound,
    Immoveable are grown:
  The fatal Goodwin swallows All that come
  Within the Limits of that dangerous Sand,
  Amphibious in its kind, nor Sea nor Land,
  Yet kin to both, a false and faithless Strand,
Known only to our Cost for a devouring Tomb.
   Nor seemed the HURRICANE content,
  Whilst only Ships were wreckt, and Tackle rent;
   The Sailors too must fall a Prey,
  Those that Command, with those that did Obey;
  The best Supporters of thy pompous Stile,
  Thou far Renown'd, thou pow'rful BRITISH Isle!
Foremost in Naval Strength, and Sov'reign of the Sea!
  These from thy Aid that wrathful Night divides,
  Plung'd in those Waves, o'er which this Title rides.

  What art Thou, envy'd Greatness, at the best,
   In thy deluding Splendors drest?
  What are thy glorious Titles, and thy Forms?
  Which cannot give Security, or Rest
  To favour'd Men, or Kingdoms that contest
With Popular Assaults, or Providential Storms!
  Whilst on th'Omnipotent our Fate depends,
And They are only safe, whom He alone defends.
  Then let to Heaven our general Praise be sent,
Which did our farther Loss, our total Wreck prevent.
  And as our Aspirations do ascend,
  Let every Thing be summon'd to attend;
  And let the Poet after God's own Heart
  Direct our Skill in that sublimer part,
   And our weak Numbers mend!

The HYMN

To the Almighty on his radiant Throne,
  Let endless Hallelujas rise!
  Praise Him, ye wondrous Heights to us unknown,
  Praise Him, ye Heavens unreach'd by mortal Eyes,
Praise Him, in your degree, ye sublunary Skies!

  Praise Him, you Angels that before him bow,
  You Creatures of Celestial frame,

Our Guests of old, our wakeful Guardians now,
    Praise Him, and with like Zeal our Hearts enflame,
Transporting then our Praise to Seats from whence you came!

    Praise Him, thou Sun in thy Meridian Force;
        Exalt Him, all ye Stars and Light!
    Praise Him, thou Moon in thy revolving Course,
        Praise Him, thou gentler Guide of silent Night,
Which do's to solemn Praise, and serious Thoughts invite.

    Praise Him, ye humid Vapours, which remain
        Unfrozen by the sharper Air;
    Praise Him, as you return in Show'rs again,
        To bless the Earth and make her Pastures fair:
Praise Him, ye climbing Fires, the Emblems of our Pray'r.

    Praise Him, ye Waters petrify'd above,
        Ye shredded Clouds that fall in Snow,
    Praise Him, for that you so divided move;
        Ye Hailstones, that you do no larger grow.
Nor, in one solid Mass, oppress the World below.

    Praise Him, ye soaring Fowls, still as you fly,
        And on gay Plumes your Bodies raise;
    You Insects, which in dark Recesses lie,
        Altho' th' extremest Distances you try,
Be reconcil'd in This, to offer mutual Praise.

    Praise Him, thou Earth, with thy unbounded Store;
        Ye Depths which to the Center tend:
    Praise Him ye Beasts which in the Forests roar;
        Praise Him ye Serpents, tho' you downwards bend,
Who made your bruised Head our Ladder to ascend.

    Praise Him, ye Men whom youthful Vigour warms;
        Ye Children, hast'ning to your Prime;
    Praise Him, ye Virgins of unsullied Charms,
        With beauteous Lips becoming sacred Rhime:
You Aged, give Him Praise for your encrease of Time.

    Praise Him, ye Monarchs in supreme Command,
        By Anthems, like the Hebrew Kings;
    Then with enlarged Zeal throughout the Land
        Reform the Numbers, and reclaim the Strings,
Converting to His Praise, the most Harmonious Things.

    Ye Senators presiding by our Choice,
        And You Hereditary Peers!

Praise Him by Union, both in Heart and Voice;
   Praise Him, who your agreeing Council steers,
Producing sweeter Sounds than the according Spheres.

   Praise Him, ye native Altars of the Earth!
      Ye Mountains of stupendious size!
   Praise Him, ye Trees and Fruits which there have birth,
   Praise Him, ye Flames that from their Bowels rise,
All fitted for the use of grateful Sacrifice.

   He spake the Word; and from the Chaos rose
      The Forms and Species of each Kind:
   He spake the Word, which did their Law compose,
   And all, with never ceasing Order join'd,
Till ruffl'd for our Sins by his chastising Wind.

   But now, you Storms, that have your Fury spent,
      As you his Dictates did obey,
   Let now your loud and threatning Notes relent,
   Tune all your Murmurs to a softer Key,
And bless that Gracious Hand, that did your Progress stay.

   From my contemn'd Retreat, obscure and low,
      As Grots from when the Winds disperse,
   May this His Praise as far extended flow;
   And if that future Times shall read my Verse,
Tho' worthless in it self, let them his Praise rehearse.

Friendship Between EPHELIA and ARDELIA

EPHELIA
What Friendship is, ARDELIA shew.

ARDELIA
'Tis to love, as I love You.

EPHELIA
This Account, so short (tho' kind)
   Suits not my enquiring Mind.

   Therefore farther now repeat;
   What is Friendship when compleat?

ARDELIA
'Tis to share all Joy and Grief;
   'Tis to lend all due Relief

From the Tongue, the Heart, the Hand;
'Tis to mortgage House and Land;
For a Friend be sold a Slave;
'Tis to die upon a Grave,
If a Friend therein do lie.

EPHELIA

This indeed, tho' carry'd high,
  This, tho' more than e'er was done
  Underneath the rolling Sun,
  This has all been said before.
  Can ARDELIA say no more?

ARDELIA

Words indeed no more can shew:
  But 'tis to love, as I love you.

The LYON and the GNAT

To the still Covert of a Wood
    About the prime of Day,
A Lyon, satiated with Food,
With stately Pace, and sullen Mood,
    Now took his lazy way.

To Rest he there himself compos'd,
    And in his Mind revolv'd,
How Great a Person it enclos'd,
How free from Danger he repos'd,
    Though now in Ease dissolv'd!

Who Guard, nor Centinel did need,
    Despising as a Jest
All whom the Forest else did feed,
As Creatures of an abject Breed,
    Who durst not him molest.

But in the Air a Sound he heard,
    That gave him some dislike;
At which he shook his grisly Beard,
Enough to make the Woods affeard,
    And stretch'd his Paw to strike.

When on his lifted Nose there fell
    A Creature, slight of Wing,
Who neither fear'd his Grin, nor Yell,

Nor Strength, that in his Jaws did dwell,
   But gores him with her Sting.

Transported with th' Affront and Pain,
   He terribly exclaims,
Protesting, if it comes again,
Its guilty Blood the Grass shall stain.
   And to surprize it aims.

The scoffing Gnat now laugh'd aloud,
   And bids him upwards view
The Jupiter within the Cloud,
That humbl'd him, who was so proud,
   And this sharp Thunder threw.

That Taunt no Lyon's Heart cou'd bear;
   And now much more he raves,
Whilst this new Perseus in the Air
Do's War and Strife again declare,
   And all his Terrour braves.

Upon his haughty Neck she rides,
   Then on his lashing Tail;
(Which need not now provoke his Sides)
Where she her slender Weapon guides,
   And makes all Patience fail.

A Truce at length he must propose,
   The Terms to be her Own;
Who likewise Rest and Quiet chose,
Contented now her Life to close,
   When she'd such Triumph known.

You mighty Men, who meaner ones despise,
Learn from this Fable to become more Wise;
You see the Lyon may be vext with Flies.

The MAN and his HORSE

Within a Meadow, on the way,
A sordid Churl resolv'd to stay,
   And give his Horse a Bite;
Purloining so his Neighbours Hay,
That at the Inn he might not pay
   For Forage all the Night.

With Heart's content th' unloaded Steed
Began to neigh, and frisk, and feed;
   For nothing more he car'd,
Since none of all his Master's breed
E'er found such Pasture, at their need,
   Or half so well had far'd.

When, in the turning of a Hand,
Out comes the Owner of the Land,
   And do's the Trespass eye;
Which puts poor Bayard to a Stand,
For now his Master do's command
   Him to return and fly.

But Hunger quick'ning up his Wit,
And Grass being sweeter than the Bit,
   He to the Clown reply'd;
Shall I for you this Dinner quit,
Who to my Back hard Burdens fit,
   And to the Death wou'd ride?

No; shou'd I as a Stray be found,
And seiz'd upon forbidden Ground,
   I'll on this Spot stand still;
For tho' new Riders shou'd abound,
(Or did Mankind this Field surround)
   They cou'd but use me ill.

Urge no Man to despair; lest in the Fit
He with some Counterblow thy Head may hit.

LIFE's Progress

How gayly is at first begun
  Our Life's uncertain Race!
Whilst yet that sprightly Morning Sun,
With which we just set out to run
  Enlightens all the Place.

How smiling the World's Prospect lies
  How tempting to go through!
Not Canaan to the Prophet's Eyes,
From Pisgah with a sweet Surprize,
  Did more inviting shew.

How promising's the Book of Fate,

Till thoroughly understood!
Whilst partial Hopes such Lots create,
As may the youthful Fancy treat
  With all that's Great and Good.

How soft the first Ideas prove,
  Which wander through our Minds!
How full the Joys, how free the Love,
Which do's that early Season move;
  As Flow'rs the Western Winds!

Our Sighs are then but Vernal Air;
  But April–drops our Tears,
Which swiftly passing, all grows Fair,
Whilst Beauty compensates our Care,
  And Youth each Vapour clears.

But oh! too soon, alas, we climb;
  Scarce feeling we ascend
The gently rising Hill of Time,
From whence with Grief we see that Prime,
  And all its Sweetness end.

The Die now cast, our Station known,
  Fond Expectation past;
The Thorns, which former Days had sown,
To Crops of late Repentance grown,
  Thro' which we toil at last.

Whilst ev'ry Care's a driving Harm,
  That helps to bear us down;
Which faded Smiles no more can charm,
But ev'ry Tear's a Winter-Storm,
  And ev'ry Look's a Frown.

Till with succeeding Ills opprest,
  For Joys we hop'd to find;
By Age too, rumpl'd and undrest,
We gladly sinking down to rest,
  Leave following Crouds behind.

HOPE

The Tree of Knowlege we in Eden prov'd;
The Tree of Life was thence to Heav'n remov'd:
Hope is the growth of Earth, the only Plant,

Which either Heav'n, or Paradice cou'd want.

Hell knows it not, to Us alone confin'd,
And Cordial only to the Human Mind.
Receive it then, t'expel these mortal Cares,
Nor wave a Med'cine, which thy God prepares.

Moral SONG

Would we attain the happiest State,
   That is design'd us here;
No Joy a Rapture must create,
   No Grief beget Despair.
No Injury fierce Anger raise,
   No Honour tempt to Pride;
No vain Desires of empty Praise
   Must in the Soul abide.
No Charms of Youth, or Beauty move
   The constant, settl'd Breast:
Who leaves a Passage free to Love,
   Shall let in, all the rest.

In such a Heart soft Peace will live,
   Where none of these abound;
The greatest Blessing, Heav'n do's give,
   Or can on Earth be found.

GLASS

O Man! what Inspiration was thy Guide,
Who taught thee Light and Air thus to divide;
To let in all the useful Beams of Day,
Yet force, as subtil Winds, without thy Shash to stay;
T'extract from Embers by a strange Device,
Then polish fair these Flakes of solid Ice;
Which, silver'd o'er, redouble all in place,
And give thee back thy well or ill-complexion'd Face.
To Vessels blown exceed the gloomy Bowl,
Which did the Wine's full excellence controul,
These shew the Body, whilst you taste the Soul.
Its colour sparkles Motion, lets thee see,
Tho' yet th' Excess the Preacher warns to flee,
Lest Men at length as clearly spy through Thee.

The DOG and his MASTER

No better Dog e'er kept his Master's Door
Than honest Snarl, who spar'd nor Rich nor Poor;
But gave the Alarm, when any one drew nigh,
Nor let pretended Friends pass fearless by:
For which reprov'd, as better Fed than Taught,
He rightly thus expostulates the Fault.
  To keep the House from Rascals was my Charge;
The Task was great, and the Commission large.
Nor did your Worship e'er declare your Mind,
That to the begging Crew it was confin'd;
Who shrink an Arm, or prop an able Knee,
Or turn up Eyes, till they're not seen, nor see.
To Thieves, who know the Penalty of Stealth,
And fairly stake their Necks against your Wealth,
These are the known Delinquents of the Times,
And Whips and Tyburn. testify their Crimes.

But since to Me there was by Nature lent
An exquisite Discerning by the Scent;
I trace a Flatt'rer, when he fawns and leers,
A rallying Wit, when he commends and jeers:
The greedy Parasite I grudging note,
Who praises the good Bits, that oil his Throat;
I mark the Lady, you so fondly toast,
That plays your Gold, when all her own is lost:
The Knave, who fences your Estate by Law,
Yet still reserves an undermining Flaw.
These and a thousand more, which I cou'd tell,
Provoke my Growling, and offend my Smell.

The PHOENIX

A SONG

A Female Friend advis'd a Swain
  (Whose Heart she wish'd at ease)
Make Love thy Pleasure, not thy Pain,
  Nor let it deeply seize.

Beauty, where Vanities abound,
  No serious Passion claims;
Then, 'till a Phoenix can be found,

Do not admit the Flames.

But griev'd She finds, that his Replies
  (Since prepossess'd when Young)
Take all their Hints from Silvia's Eyes,
  None from ARDELIA's Tongue.

Thus, Cupid, of our Aim we miss,
  Who wou'd unbend thy Bow;
And each slight Nymph a Phoenix is,
  When Love will have it so.

A SONG

Persuade me not, there is a Grace
  Proceeds from Silvia's Voice or Lute,
Against Miranda's charming Face
  To make her hold the least Dispute.

Musick, which tunes the Soul for Love,
  And stirs up all our soft Desires,
Do's but the glowing Flame improve,
  Which pow'rful Beauty first inspires.

Thus, whilst with Art she plays, and sings
  I to Miranda, standing by,
Impute the Music of the Strings,
  And all the melting Words apply.

JEALOUSY

A Song

Vain Love, why do'st thou boast of Wings,
  That cannot help thee to retire!
When such quick Flames Suspicion brings,
  As do the Heart about thee fire.
Still Swift to come, but when to go
Thou shou'd'st be more—Alas! how Slow.

Lord of the World must surely be
  But thy bare Title at the most;
Since Jealousy is Lord of Thee,
  And makes such Havock on thy Coast,

As do's thy pleasant Land deface,
Yet binds thee faster to the Place.

A SONG

Love, thou art best of Human Joys,
  Our chiefest Happiness below;
All other Pleasures are but Toys,
Musick without Thee is but Noise,
  And Beauty but an empty Show.
Heav'n, who knew best what Man wou'd move,
  And raise his Thoughts above the Brute;
Said, Let him Be, and let him Love;
That must alone his Soul improve,
  Howe'er Philosophers dispute.

A SONG

Quickly, Delia, Learn my Passion,
  Lose not Pleasure, to be Proud;
Courtship draws on Observation,
  And the Whispers of the Croud.

Soon or late you'll hear a Lover,
  Nor by Time his Truth can prove;
Ages won't a Heart discover,
  Trust, and so secure my Love.

A SONG

'TIS strange, this Heart within my breast,
  Reason opposing, and her Pow'rs,
Cannot one gentle Moment rest,
  Unless it knows what's done in Yours.

In vain I ask it of your Eyes,
  Which subt'ly would my Fears controul;
For Art has taught them to disguise,
  Which Nature made t' explain the Soul.

In vain that Sound, your Voice affords,
  Flatters sometimes my easy Mind;

But of too vast Extent are Words
  In them the Jewel Truth to find.

Then let my fond Enquiries cease,
  And so let all my Troubles end:
For, sure, that Heart shall ne'er know Peace,
  Which on Anothers do's depend.

To Mr. F. Now Earl of W.

Who going abroad, had desired ARDELIA to write some Verses upon whatever Subject she thought fit, against his Return in the Evening

Written in the Year 1689

No sooner, FLAVIO, was you gone,
But, your Injunction thought upon,
  ARDELIA took the Pen;
Designing to perform the Task,
Her FLAVIO did so kindly ask,
  Ere he returned agen.

Unto Parnassus strait she sent,
And bid the Messenger, that went
  Unto the Muses Court,
Assure them, she their Aid did need,
And begg'd they'd use their utmost Speed,
  Because the Time was short.

The hasty Summons was allow'd;
And being well-bred, they rose and bow'd,
  And said, they'd poste away;
That well they did ARDELIA know,
And that no Female's Voice below
  They sooner wou'd obey:

That many of that rhiming Train,
On like Occasions, sought in vain
  Their Industry t'excite;
But for ARDELIA all they'd leave:
Thus flatt'ring can the Muse deceive,
  And wheedle us to write.

Yet, since there was such haste requir'd;
To know the Subject 'twas desir'd,
  On which they must infuse;

That they might temper Words and Rules,
And with their Counsel carry Tools,
  As Country-Doctors use.

Wherefore to cut off all Delays,
'Twas soon reply'd, a Husband's Praise
  (Tho' in these looser Times)
ARDELIA gladly wou'd rehearse
A Husband's, who indulg'd her Verse,
  And now requir'd her Rimes.

A Husband! eccho'd all around:
And to Parnassus sure that Sound
  Had never yet been sent;
Amazement in each Face was read,
In haste th'affrighted Sisters fled,
  And unto Council went.

Erato cry'd, since Grizel's Days,
Since Troy-Town pleas'd, and Chivey-chace,
  No such Design was known;
And 'twas their Bus'ness to take care,
It reach'd not to the publick Ear,
  Or got about the Town:

Nor came where Evening Beaux were met
O'er Billet-doux and Chocolate,
  Lest it destroy'd the House;
For in that Place, who cou'd dispence
(That wore his Cloaths with common Sense)
  With mention of a Spouse?

'Twas put unto the Vote at last,
And in the Negative it past,
  None to her Aid shou'd move;
Yet since ARDELIA was a Friend,
Excuses 'twas agreed to send,
  Which plausible might prove:

That Pegasus of late had been
So often rid thro' thick and thin,
  With neither Fear nor Wit;
In Panegyrick been so spurr'd
He cou'd not from the Stall be stirr'd,
  Nor wou'd endure the Bit.

Melpomene had given a Bond,
By the new House alone to stand,

And write of War and Strife;
Thalia, she had taken Fees,
And Stipends from the Patentees,
  And durst not for her Life.

Urania only lik'd the Choice;
Yet not to thwart the publick Voice,
  She whisp'ring did impart:
They need no Foreign Aid invoke,
No help to draw a moving Stroke,
  Who dictate from the Heart.

Enough! the pleas'd ARDELIA cry'd;
And slighting ev'ry Muse beside,
  Consulting now her Breast,
Perceiv'd that ev'ry tender Thought,
Which from abroad she'd vainly sought,
  Did there in Silence rest:

And shou'd unmov'd that Post maintain,
Till in his quick Return again,
  Met in some neighb'ring Grove,
(Where Vice nor Vanity appear)
Her FLAVIO them alone might hear,
  In all the Sounds of Love.

For since the World do's so despise
Hymen's Endearments and its Ties,
  They shou'd mysterious be;
Till We that Pleasure too possess
(Which makes their fancy'd Happiness)
  Of stollen Secrecy.

A LETTER to the Same Person

Sure of Success, to You I boldly write,
Whilst Love do's ev'ry tender Line endite;
Love, who is justly President of Verse,
Which all his Servants write, or else rehearse.
Phoebus (howe'er mistaken Poets dream)
Ne'er us'd a Verse, till Love became his Theme.
To his stray'd Son, still as his Passion rose,
He rais'd his hasty Voice in clam'rous Prose:
But when in Daphne he wou'd Love inspire,
He woo'd in Verse, set to his silver Lyre.
  The Trojan Prince did pow'rful Numbers join

To sing of War; but Love was the Design:
And sleeping Troy again in Flames was drest,
To light the Fires in pitying Dido's Breast.
  Love without Poetry's refining Aid
Is a dull Bargain, and but coarsely made;
Nor e'er cou'd Poetry successful prove,
Or touch the Soul, but when the Sense was Love.
  Oh! cou'd they both In Absence now impart
Skill to my Hand, but to describe my Heart;
Then shou'd you see impatient of your Stay
Soft Hopes contend with Fears of sad Delay;
Love in a thousand fond Endearments there,
And lively Images of You appear.
But since the Thoughts of a Poetick Mind
Will never be to Syllables confin'd;
And whilst to fix what is conceiv'd, we try,
The purer Parts evaporate and dye:
You must perform what they want force to do,
And think what your ARDELIA thinks of you.

October 21, 1690.

FRAGMENT

So here confin'd, and but to female Clay,
ARDELIA's Soul mistook the rightful Way:
Whilst the soft Breeze of Pleasure's tempting Air
Made her believe, Felicity was there;
And basking in the warmth of early Time,
To vain Amusements dedicate her Prime.
Ambition next allur'd her tow'ring Eye;
For Paradice she heard was plac'd on high,
Then thought, the Court with all its glorious Show
Was sure above the rest, and Paradice below.
There plac'd too soon the flaming Sword appear'd,
Remov'd those Pow'rs, whom justly she rever'd,
Adher'd too in their Wreck, and in their Ruin shar'd.
Now by the Wheels inevitable Round,
With them thrown prostrate to the humble Ground,
No more she takes (instructed by that Fall)
For fix'd, or worth her thought, this rolling Ball:
Tow'rds a more certain Station she aspires,
Unshaken by Revolts, and owns no less Desires.
But all in vain are Pray'rs, extatick Thoughts,
Recover'd Moments, and retracted Faults,
Retirement, which the World Moroseness calls,

Abandon'd Pleasures in Monastick Walls:
These, but at distance, towards that purpose tend,
The lowly Means to an exalted End;
Which He must perfect, who allots her Stay,
And That, accomplish'd, will direct the way.
Pity her restless Cares, and weary Strife,
And point some Issue to escaping Life;
Which so dismiss'd, no Pen or Human Speech
Th' ineffable Recess can ever teach:
Th' Expanse, the Light, the Harmony, the Throng,
The Bride's Attendance, and the Bridal Song,
The numerous Mansions, and th' immortal Tree,
No Eye, unpurg'd by Death, must ever see,
Or Waves which through that wond'rous City roll.
Rest then content, my too impatient Soul;
Observe but here the easie Precepts given,
Then wait with chearful hope, till Heaven be known in Heaven.

PSALM the 137th Paraphras'd to the 7th Verse

Proud Babylon! Thou saw'st us weep;
  Euphrates, as he pass'd along,
Saw, on his Banks, the Sacred Throng
  A heavy, solemn Mourning keep.
Sad Captives to thy Sons, and Thee,
When nothing but our Tears were Free!

A Song of Sion they require,
  And from the neighb'ring Trees to take
Each Man his dumb, neglected Lyre,
  And chearful Sounds on them awake:
But chearful Sounds the Strings refuse,
Nor will their Masters Griefs abuse.

How can We, Lord, thy Praise proclaim,
  Here, in a strange unhallow'd Land!
Lest we provoke them to Blaspheme
  A Name, they do not understand;
And with rent Garments, that deplore
Above whate'er we felt before.

But, Thou, Jerusalem, so Dear!
  If thy lov'd Image e'er depart,
Or I forget thy Suff'rings here;
  Let my right Hand forget her Art;
My Tongue her vocal Gift resign,

And Sacred Verse no more be mine!

The Battle Between the Rats and the Weazles

In dire Contest the Rats and Weazles met,
And Foot to Foot, and Point to Point was set.
An ancient Quarrel had such Hatred wrought,
That for Revenge, as for Renown, they fought.
Now bloody was the Day, and hard the Strife,
Wherein bold Warriors lost neglected Life;
But as, some Errors still we must commit,
Nor Valour always ballanc'd is by Wit;
Among the Rats some Officers appear'd,
With lofty Plumage on their Foreheads rear'd,
Unthinking they, and ruin'd by their Pride:
For when the Weazles prov'd the stronger Side,
A gen'ral Rout befell, and a Retreat,
Was by the Vanquish'd now implor'd of Fate;
To slender Crannies all repair'd in haste,
Where easily the undress'd Vulgar past:
But when the Rats of Figure wou'd have fled,
So wide those branching Marks of Honour spread,
The Feather in the Cap was fatal to the Head.

Democritus and His Neighbors

Imitated from Fontaine

In Vulgar Minds what Errors do arise!
How diff'ring are the Notions, they possess,
  From theirs, whom better Sense do's bless,
Who justly are enroll'd amongst the Learn'd and Wise!
Democritus, whilst he all Science taught,
  Was by his foolish Neighbors thought
    Distracted in his Wits;
  Who call his speculative Flights,
  His solitary Walks in starry Nights,
    But wild and frantick Fits.
Bless me, each cries, from such a working Brain!
  And to Hippocrates they send
  The Sage's long-acquainted Friend,
To put in Tune his jarring Mind again,
    And Pericranium mend.

Away the Skilful Doctor comes
  Of Recipes and Med'cines full,
To check the giddy Whirl of Nature's Fires,
  If so th' unruly Case requires;
Or with his Cobweb-cleansing Brooms
To sweep and clear the over-crouded Scull,
If settl'd Spirits flag, and make the Patient dull.
  But asking what the Symptoms were,
  That made 'em think he was so bad?
  The Man indeed, they cry'd, is wond'rous Mad.
You, at this Distance, may behold him there
  Beneath that Tree in open Air,
Surrounded with the Engines of his Fate,
  The Gimcracks of a broken Pate.
   Those Hoops a Sphere he calls,
   That Ball the Earth;
And when into his raving Fit he falls,
'Twou'd move at once your Pity, and your Mirth,
  To hear him, as you will do soon,
Declaring, there's a Kingdom in the Moon;
  And that each Star, for ought he knows,
  May some Inhabitants enclose:
Philosophers, he says, may there abound,
Such Jugglers as himself be in them found;
Which if there be, the World may well turn round;
  At least to those, whose Whimsies are so strange,
  That, whilst they're fixt to one peculiar Place,
  Pretend to measure far extended Space,
  And 'mongst the Planets range.
  Behold him now contemplating that Head,
From which long-since both Flesh, and Brains are fled;
Questioning, if that empty, hollow Bowl
Did not ere while contain the Human Soul:
Then starts a Doubt, if 't were not to the Heart
That Nature rather did that Gift impart.
Good Sir, employ the utmost of your Skill,
To make him Wiser, tho' against his Will;
Who thinks, that he already All exceeds,
And laughs at our most solemn Words and Deeds:
Tho' once amongst us he wou'd try a Cause,
  And Bus'ness of the Town discuss,
  Knowing as well as one of us,
The Price of Corn, and standing Market-Laws;
  Wou'd bear an Office in his Turn,
For which good Purposes all Men were born;
Not to be making Circles in the Sand,
And scaling Heav'n, till they have sold their Land;
Or, when unstock'd below their Pasture lies,

To find out Bulls and Rams, amidst the Skies.
From these Mistakes his Madness we conclude;
And hearing, you was with much Skill endu'd,
Your Aid we sought. Hippocrates amaz'd,
Now on the Sage, now on the Rabble gaz'd;
And whilst he needless finds his artful Rules,
Pities a Man of Sense, judg'd by a Croud of Fools.
Then how can we with their Opinions join,
Who, to promote some Int'rest, wou'd define
The People's Voice to be the Voice Divine?

The Tree

Fair Tree! for thy delightful Shade
'Tis just that some Return be made:
Sure, some Return is due from me
To thy cool Shadows, and to thee.
When thou to Birds do'st Shelter give,
Thou Music do'st from them receive;
If Travellers beneath thee stay,
Till Storms have worn themselves away,
That Time in praising thee they spend,
And thy protecting Pow'r commend:
The Shepherd here, from Scorching freed,
Tunes to thy dancing Leaves his Reed;
Whilst his lov'd Nymph, in Thanks, bestows
Her flow'ry Chaplets on thy Boughs.
Shall I then only Silent be,
And no Return be made by me?
No; let this Wish upon thee wait,
And still to flourish be thy Fate,
To future Ages may'st thou stand
Untouch'd by the rash Workman's hand;
'Till that large Stock of Sap is spent,
Which gives thy Summer's Ornament;
'Till the fierce Winds, that vainly strive
To shock thy Greatness whilst alive,
Shall on thy lifeless Hour attend,
Prevent the Axe, and grace thy End;
Their scatter'd Strength together call
And to the Clouds proclaim thy Fall;
Who then their Ev'ning-Dews may spare,
When thou no longer art their Care,
But shalt, like ancient Heroes, burn,
And some bright Hearth be made thy Urn.

A Nocturnal Reverie

In such a Night, when every louder Wind
Is to its distant Cavern safe confin'd;
And only gentle Zephyr fans his Wings,
And lonely Philomel, still waking, sings;
Or from some Tree, fam'd for the Owl's delight,
She, hollowing clear, directs the Wand'rer right:
In such a Night, when passing Clouds give place,
Or thinly vail the Heav'ns mysterious Face;
When in some River, overhung with Green,
The waving Moon and trembling Leaves are seen;
When freshen'd Grass now bears it self upright,
And makes cool Banks to pleasing Rest invite,
Whence springs the Woodbind, and the Bramble–Rose,
And where the sleepy Cowslip shelter'd grows;
Whilst now a paler Hue the Foxglove takes,
Yet checquers still with Red the dusky brakes:
When scattered Glow-worms, but in Twilight fine,
Shew trivial Beauties watch their Hour to shine;
Whilst Salisb'ry stands the Test of every Light,
In perfect Charms, and perfect Virtue bright:
When Odours, which declin'd repelling Day,
Thro' temp'rate Air uninterrupted stray;
When darken'd Groves their softest Shadows wear,
And falling Waters we distinctly hear;
When thro' the Gloom more venerable shows
Some ancient Fabrick, awful in Repose,
While Sunburnt Hills their swarthy Looks conceal,
And swelling Haycocks thicken up the Vale:
When the loos'd Horse now, as his Pasture leads,
Comes slowly grazing thro' th' adjoining Meads,
Whose stealing Pace and lengthen'd Shade we fear,
Till torn up Forage in his Teeth we hear:
When nibbling Sheep at large pursue their Food,
And unmolested Kine rechew the Cud;
When Curlews cry beneath the Village-walls,
And to her straggling Brood the Partridge calls;
Their shortliv'd Jubilee the Creatures keep,
Which but endures, whilst Tyrant-Man do's sleep;
When a sedate Content the Spirit feels,
And no fierce Light disturbs, whilst it reveals;
But silent Musings urge the Mind to seek
Something, too high for Syllables to speak;
Till the free Soul, to a compos'dness charm'd,
Finding the Elements of Rage disarm'd,

O'er all below a solemn Quiet grown,
Joys in th' inferiour World and thinks it like her Own:
In such a Night let Me abroad remain,
Till Morning breaks, and All's contus'd again;
Our Cares, our Toils, our Clamours are renew'd,
Or Pleasures, seldom reach'd, again pursu'd.

Anne Kingsmill Finch – A Short Biography

Anne Kingsmill was born in April 1661 (an exact date is not known) in Sydmonton, Hampshire. Her parents; Sir William Kingsmill and Anne Haslewood were both from rich and powerful families. Anne was the youngest of three children. When she was only five months her father died but his will stipulated that his daughters receive the same financial support as their brother for education. An unusually enlightened view for the times.

Her mother remarried in 1662, to Sir Thomas Ogle, and later bore Anne's half-sister, Dorothy Ogle, but sadly in 1664 her mother then died. Her will gave control of her estate to her second husband. This was successfully challenged in a Court of Chancery by Anne's uncle, William Haslewood. Subsequently, Anne and her sister Bridget lived with their grandmother, Lady Kingsmill, in Charing Cross, London, while their brother lived with his uncle, William Haslewood.

In 1670, Lady Kingsmill filed her own Court of Chancery suit, requiring a share in the educational and support monies for Anne and Bridget. The court split custody and financial support between Haslewood and Lady Kingsmill. When Lady Kingsmill died in 1672, Anne and Bridget rejoined their brother to be raised by Haslewood.

The sisters received a comprehensive and progressive education, something that was uncommon for females at the time, and Anne learned about Greek and Roman mythology, the Bible, French and Italian languages, history, poetry, and drama.

In 1682, Anne was sent to St James's Palace to become a maid of honour to Mary of Modena (wife of James, Duke of York, later King James II).

Anne's interest in poetry began at the palace, and she started writing her own verse. Her friends included Sarah Churchill and Anne Killigrew, two other maids of honour with poetic interests. However, when Anne witnessed the derision that greeted Killigrew's poetic efforts (a pursuit not considered suitable for women), she decided to keep her own writing attempts to herself and her close friends. This view was to remain with her until much later in life.

While residing at court, Anne met Colonel Heneage Finch. A courtier as well as a soldier, Finch had been appointed Groom of the Bedchamber to James, Duke of York, in 1683. His family had strong Royalist connections, as well as a pronounced loyalty to the Stuart dynasty. Finch fell in love with Anne who at first resisted but Finch proved a persistent and successful suitor.

The couple married on 15th May 1684 and Anne resigned her court position. Her husband retained his own appointment and would also serve in various government positions. The couple were determined to remain involved in court life.

The marriage was enduring and happy, in part due to the equality in their partnership. Her poetic skills blossomed as she expressed her love for her husband and the positive effects of his support on her artistic development.

Their life was rather sedate but when James II took the throne Heneage became more involved in public affairs. The couple were very loyal to the king in what turned out to be a brief reign. James II was deposed in 1688 during the "Bloodless Revolution" when William of Orange was offered the English crown. When the new monarchs, William and Mary, both Protestants, assumed the throne, oaths of allegiance were required from both the public and the clergy. The Finches refused to take the oath and remained loyal to the Catholic Stuart court. This invited trouble. Heneage lost his government position, his income and retreated from public life. The Finches were forced to live with friends in London where they faced harassment, fines and the threat of imprisonment.

In April 1690, Heneage was arrested and charged with Jacobitism. Heneage and Anne would remain separated from April until November of that year. This caused the couple a great deal of emotional turmoil. Anne often fell ill to bouts of depression, something that afflicted her for most of her adult life. Her work was noticeably less playful than her earlier poems.

After Finch was released and his case dismissed, his nephew Charles Finch, the fourth Earl of Winchelsea, invited them to move into the family estate at Eastwell Park, Kent. The Finches took up residence in late 1690 and found peace and security. They would reside there for the next 25 years.

For Anne the estate provided fertile ground for her literary efforts which were encouraged by both Charles and Heneage. Her husband's support was also practical. He collected a portfolio of her 56 poems, writing them out by hand and made small changes. One significant change involved her pen name, which he changed from "Areta" to "Ardelia".

King William died in 1702, and his death was followed by the succession of Queen Anne, the daughter of James II (who had died the previous year). With these developments, the Finches felt ready to embrace a more public lifestyle. Finch ran for parliament three times (in 1701, 1705, and 1710), but was never elected. Still, they now felt ready to leave the country and move to London.

In London, Anne was encouraged to publish her poetry. In 1701 she published "The Spleen" anonymously. This well-received reflection on depression would prove to be her most popular poem.

Anne also acquired some influential friends, including Jonathan Swift and Alexander Pope, who encouraged her to write and publish much more openly. She was reluctant, as she felt the climate still remained oppressive for women. When she published 'Miscellany Poems, on Several Occasions' in 1713, the cover page of the first printing stated that the work was "Written by a Lady." On subsequent printings, she received credit as Anne, Countess of Winchilsea.

Anne became Countess of Winchilsea upon the sudden and unexpected death of the childless Charles Finch on 4th August 1712. However, the titles came with a cost. They had to assume and discharge

Charles Finch's financial and legal burdens. This was eventually settled in the Finches' favour, after seven years of further emotional strain, in 1720.

They also faced renewed strains from court politics. When Queen Anne died in 1714, she was succeeded by George I. Subsequently, a Whig government, hostile to the Jacobite cause, came to power. The Jacobite rebellion of 1715, further aggravated the political situation. They were now concerned for their safety.

These and other worries combined started to take a toll on Anne's health, which began to deteriorate. In 1715 she became seriously ill. Her later poems spoke of this. In particular, 'A Suplication for the Joys of Heaven' and 'A Contemplation' expressed her concerns about her life, political and spiritual beliefs.

Anne Kingsmill-Finch died on August 5th 1720 in Westminster, London. Her body was returned to Eastwell for burial, according to her previously stated wishes.

In her obituary her husband praised her talents as a writer and her virtues as an individual. A portion of it read, "To draw her Ladyship's just Character, requires a masterly Pen like her own (She being a fine Writer, and an excellent Poet); we shall only presume to say, she was the most faithful Servant to her Royall Mistresse, the best Wife to her Noble Lord, and in every other Relation, publick and private, so illustrious an Example of such extraordinary Endowments, both of Body and Mind, that the Court of England never bred a more accomplished Lady, nor the Church of England a better Christian."

Anne Kingsmill Finch – A Concise Bibliography

Upon the Death of King James the Second (1701)
The Tunbridge Prodigy (1706)
The Spleen, A Pindarique Ode. By a Lady (1709)
Free-thinkers: A Poem in Dialogue (1711)
Miscellany Poems, on Several Occasions. Written by a Lady (1713)

Editions and Collections
The Poems of Anne Countess of Winchilsea, edited by Myra Reynolds (1903)
Selected Poems of Anne Finch, Countess of Winchilsea (1906)
Poems, by Anne, Countess of Winchilsea, compiled by John Middleton Murry (1928)

www.ingramcontent.com/pod-product-compliance
Lightning Source LLC
LaVergne TN
LVHW091224080426
835509LV00009B/1158